* * * *

VANITY FAIR'S
PRESIDENTIAL
PROFILES

* * * * * * * * * * * * * * *

———

VANITY FAIR'S
PRESIDENTIAL
PROFILES

———

Edited, and with an Introduction, by
GRAYDON CARTER

Illustrations by
MARK SUMMERS

Foreword by
TODD S. PURDUM

– *Essays by* –

JUDY BACHRACH

DAVID FRIEND

DAVID KAMP

TODD S. PURDUM

and

JIM WINDOLF

* * * * * * * * * * * * * * *

Design by David Harris and Piper Vitale.
Set in Hoefler Text and Caslon.

Library of Congress Cataloging-in-Publication Data
Vanity fair's presidential profiles : defining portraits, deeds, and misdeeds of 43 notable
Americans—and what each one really thought about his predecessor /
edited and with an introduction by Graydon Carter ; illustrated by Mark Summers ;
foreword by Todd S. Purdum.
p. cm.
ISBN 978-0-8109-8487-5 (hardcover with jacket)
1. Presidents—United States—Biography. 2. Presidents—United States—Portraits.
I. Carter, Graydon. II. Summers, Mark. III. Vanity fair (New York, N.Y.)
IV. Title: Presidential profiles.
E176.1.V37 2010
973.09'9—dc22
|B| 2009033310

Printed and bound in the United States of America
10 9 8 7 6 5 4 3 2 1

ABRAMS
THE ART OF BOOKS SINCE 1949
115 West 18th Street
New York, NY 10011
www.abramsbooks.com

·The Presidents·

CONTENTS

THE PRESIDENTS

★ ★ ★

* * *

* * *

INTRODUCTION

By Graydon Carter

A few years back, Mark Summers, one of the leading illustrators of our age, decided that he wanted to do something big. And although he's Canadian, he wanted to do something big and *American* (as if there were any other kind). He wanted to create a tableau of presidential heads—all forty-four of them (well, forty-three, to be exact; Grover Cleveland served *twice,* as Nos. 22 and 24)—and all in perfectly detailed profile.

It's actually much more difficult than it sounds. The drawing part Summers could do standing on his head—if you've seen his portraits of authors for Barnes & Noble, you'll know what I mean. Whistling up reference images of all the presidents in right-side profile, on the other hand, was no simple task. (Remember that five of them served out their terms before photography was invented.) He spent a full decade just on research, chasing down sidelong references in paintings, sketches, sculpture, photos, even freeze-frame TV footage.

When Summers had done about three dozen portraits, he brought them up to the *Vanity Fair* offices and we commissioned him to complete the project on our dime. (A dime, incidentally, turned out to be one of his references, inasmuch as it features Franklin Delano Roosevelt, in profile, on its obverse side.) When he brought in completed renderings of forty-two presidents (we were waiting to see who No. 44 would be), we decided to turn his ten-year-long project into the compact volume you are now holding.

S ketching the American presidents might seem an odd hobby for a genial fellow from the provinces—I'm talking about Summers here—but he says he has always been fascinated by U.S. history and culture, especially the presidency, which he calls "a mild obsession since I was young."

Vanity Fair's interest in the White House and its occupants goes back to the magazine's first run, from 1913 to 1936. In that Jazz Age incarnation, *Vanity Fair* published stiff, resolute portraits of Woodrow Wilson, Calvin Coolidge, and Herbert Hoover, alongside text that was often less than respectful. Coolidge—"the Great Stone Face," in the magazine's words—was depicted in 1932 by the gifted caricaturist Covarrubias, looking especially prudish and fussbudgety, and glowering at a lithe, flirtatious Greta Garbo. Hoover, poor fellow, was snottily upbraided in *Vanity Fair* for his hayseed enthusiasm on a trip to New York. "There was something a little pathetic about [Hoover]," columnist Drew Pearson wrote, "getting the same kick out of Fifth Avenue window shopping as the girl from Keokuk on her first visit." F.D.R. appeared in caricature on the cover nine times—as everything from a circus ringmaster to a cowboy riding the continental U.S. as his personal hobbyhorse.

The Arthurian administration of John F. Kennedy, so resonant as it was with youth, glamour, intellectual rigor, social activism, and irrepressible aspiration, has, not surprisingly, been editorial catnip for the magazine over the years. Jack, Jackie, John junior, and Bobby Kennedy have appeared on the cover a total of eight times. Robert F. Kennedy Jr. has appeared on the cover as well—and has written movingly for us on environmental issues. We've published pieces on everything from Joe Kennedy's Hollywood years to Jackie's White House dinners and her battle to suppress passages of historian William Manchester's *The Death of a President*.

The Nixon administration was another matter. We've drawn attention to his private anti-Semitic outbursts and to the travails of his chief foreign-policy strategist, Henry Kissinger, whom *V.F.*'s own Christopher Hitchens has called a war criminal. And it was, *ahem,* the monthly *Vanity Fair*—not a daily paper, a 24-7 news channel, or a Web site—that exposed the identity of Watergate's "Deep Throat," telling the world in 2005 that F.B.I. official Mark Felt had been *The Washington Post*'s secret source during the scandal that would push Nixon from office in 1974.

In general, and for better or worse, *Vanity Fair* wholeheartedly embraced Ronald and Nancy Reagan. In the high-flying 80s, they were presented as the Mom and Pop (or Louis XVI and Marie Antoinette) of, quote unquote, Prosperity—beginning in 1985 with a glowing piece by William F. Buckley Jr. that was tethered to an iconic cover by Harry Benson showing the First Couple mid-foxtrot (the president in a dinner jacket, Mrs. Reagan in sequins). More recently, *V.F.* contributor Bob Colacello has become the virtual Boswell of the Reagans and their inner circle, writing some thirty-eight thousand words on the subject for the magazine.

Our last four presidents—from George H. W. Bush through Barack Obama—have been subjected to every manner of treatment in our pages, from encomium to excoriation, by writers as diverse as Robert Sam Anson, Leslie Bennetts, Carl Bernstein, Harold Bloom, Niall Ferguson, David Halberstam, Christopher Hitchens, Edward Klein, Cullen Murphy, Maureen Orth, Todd S. Purdum, Gail Sheehy, Sally Bedell Smith, Joseph E. Stiglitz, Gore Vidal, and Marjorie Williams. Perhaps most noteworthy of all, in terms of the magazine's influence on presidential image, is the fact that shortly after a new administration assumes office it inevitably has its date with *Vanity Fair*'s principal photographer, Annie Leibovitz. On assignment for the magazine, she took the first Oval Office portrait of Bill Clinton on the day he and his family moved into 1600 Pennsylvania Avenue. Leibovitz also shot the now famous tableau of George W. Bush's war council, in the Cabinet Room, during the 2001 Afghan invasion. And in early 2009, she produced a series of freshman-class pictures introducing forty-six key members of the incoming Obama team. Indeed, as I write this, Leibovitz has been spending a few days each month photographing the Obama family and administration in the White House.

Here, then, is another sort of *Vanity Fair* group portrait. Within these pages you will find a series of exquisite illustrations and smart, brief essays on the chosen few who have held the highest office in the land. Taken together, they present an image of power and conscience, of resolve and endurance, of brilliance and stupidity—our 21st-century rendering of the changing face of the American presidency. Hail to the chiefs.

GRAYDON CARTER
New York City, 2009

THE FACE OF POWER

BY TODD S. PURDUM

*T*he word itself derives from the Italian verb *profilare*—to outline—and from Egyptian paintings to Roman coins to Victorian paper silhouettes, the profile has been the most instantly recognizable form of portraiture, the sidelong view that tells the whole story at a glance. In the hands of a sidewalk sketch artist or a master engraver, on a copper penny just three-quarters of an inch across or on a billboard as big as a barn, it is the profile that packs the punch, projecting the sum and substance of its subject in a few spare lines. We take its impact for granted, and so are always pleasantly surprised at its effect. Not for nothing does every humble police mug shot come in two parts: the head-on view and the profile.

The profile holds a particular place in the iconography of power. Coins were cast bearing the images of Roman emperors, as symbols of the empire's wealth and reach and authority, and bas-reliefs of other monarchs down through the ages were carved into stone for much the same reason. For the first half of its history, the United States eschewed such displays as undemocratic. It was not until 1909, on the centennial of Abraham Lincoln's birth, that Theodore Roosevelt ordered Lincoln's profile placed on the penny, making him the first historical, as opposed to allegorical, figure to appear on an American coin. (A century later, the Lincoln penny has been reproduced nearly half a trillion times.)

That familiar image of Lincoln came from an equally famous 1864 profile photograph taken by Anthony Berger of Mathew Brady's studio in Washington, D.C. Brady was the reigning American photographer of his day, and his distinguished depictions of Lincoln from the 1860 campaign, one of them in profile, are credited with helping to make the gaunt rail-splitter from Illinois into a plausible presidential contender, just as Brady's photographs of Civil War battlefields helped bring the visual horrors of war into American homes for the first time.

Through the decades, the iconography of the American presidency has involved far more than profiles. From Gilbert Stuart's grand and definitive portrait of the standing George Washington to Shepard Fairey's mixed-media, collage-style, red-white-and-blue poster of Barack Obama, there have been majestic images, and humble ones, in every medium imaginable. Each president since John Quincy Adams (who sat for his first daguerreotype in old age, after leaving office) has been photographed, and every one since Benjamin Harrison has had his voice recorded. (Richard Nixon might have wished otherwise.) Since D. W. Griffith's *The Birth of a Nation,* in 1915, presidents—real and imagined—have been portrayed in scores of feature films. And in the modern media maelstrom, presidents have been sliced and diced and subjected to microscopic examination—quite literally in the case of Bill Clinton, who had his DNA tested in a criminal investigation as a result of his affair with White House intern Monica Lewinsky.

Not even the most iconic presidential portraits are always what they seem. One of the most famous images of John F. Kennedy, photographed by the late George Tames of *The New York Times,* shows him from behind, leaning over a table in the Oval Office, seemingly lost in somber contemplation of "the Loneliest Job in the World," which is what Tames called his picture. In fact, the mood in the Oval Office when Tames made the shot was quite different, he later recalled. Kennedy was examining a copy of the *Times*'s editorial pages, and reading an unflattering column by Arthur Krock. "I wonder where Mr. Krock gets all the crap he puts in this horseshit column of his," Kennedy demanded.

In Washington, there are two great collections of presidential portraits, one in the Smithsonian's National Portrait Gallery and the other in the White House itself, and the works in those archives tend to be rather grand and formal, in full color: John Singer Sargent's bracing Theodore Roosevelt, with impatient hand holding a stairway finial; George P. A. Healy's pensive Abraham Lincoln, chin in his hand as if worn down by the weight of the Civil War itself. There are exceptions: The Portrait Gallery has an oddly attractive and sympathetic Richard Nixon, painted in oil with photographic fidelity by Norman Rockwell, who confessed that he erred on the side of making Nixon look better than he usually did. Interestingly, in even the face-front portraits, the presidents' heads tend to be turned or tilted just slightly, the better to reveal a Roman nose, a jutting jaw, or a jug ear.

So there is something both refreshing and revealing about these elegant pencil sketches by Mark Summers, with the presidents arranged *en enfilade,* from No. 1 to No. 44, as if looking over each other's shoulders. (In truth, as Summers explained to me, each president's face is tilted about ten degrees toward the viewer so as to make a hint of the left eye visible.) In their very simplicity—no eagles, pedestals, pediments, or monuments—Summers's profiles allow for quiet reflection on the personalities and characters of their subjects, and the achievements and setbacks of their terms. The expressions are neutral, those of faces in repose (a luxury, it must be said, seldom afforded flesh-and-blood presidents).

Although the portraits are presented in these pages as finished works, they are in fact Summers's preliminary sketches, prepared on tracing paper so they could be placed over his usual medium: scratchboard, which has a white, waxy surface that can be scraped away to reveal solid black lines underneath. The ultimate effect is of an engraving. (Among Summers's best-known works are a series of scratchboard portraits of famous authors, commissioned by Barnes & Noble; he has also created portraits of Jonas Salk and Wilma Rudolph, among others, for United States Postal Service stamps.) Summers says that "a lot of what's happening" in these sketches is "shorthand notes." If so, the effect is telegraphic, with the portraits succinctly capturing the essence of their sitters.

Because the human eye tends to read from left to right (at least in English speakers), Summers quickly decided that the presidents should all face right, as if lined up above a schoolroom blackboard, in chronological order. But the extensive catalogue of extant presidential imagery did not really deliver the goods. "I think I only ever found five pictures of people heading in the right direction," he says. "I wound up having to shift a lot of hairstyles. What I also started to notice, when you talk about silhouettes, once you start going through these drawings, you realize it's always a decade-by-decade, two-hundred-year history of what men's shirt collars looked like. Initially, the collars are very high, with very frilly accessories. From Hoover on, you don't notice any change at all, really."

Summers generally avoided working from existing paintings, preferring to rely on sculpture whenever possible. He combed old art books, looking for faces that were in the right general position or that could be flopped. Of all the presidents, the only one for whom he could find no profile view was Martin Van Buren. "There's just absolutely nothing," he insists; so he had to improvise. Summers says he worked to keep his portraits studiously neutral. "I wanted to eliminate any hint of favoritism," he says, "so I sort of viewed these as almost medical drawings, very clinical, just to show who these people were, and try to keep expression out as much as possible. Because when you do that, the viewer will bring emotions. A lot of the most famous portraits—*American Gothic, Whistler's Mother,* the *Mona Lisa*—are devoid of expression, or almost." (Even so, I swear I see a hint of a smile crossing the lips of Summers's Barack Obama, on page 93.)

The word "profile" means the same thing with respect to prose as it does to pictures, and the brief, vivid biographical and character sketches in this volume will attest to that fact. They are outlines of great lives and great disappointments, of men for the ages and men of their times. From George Washington to George W. Bush and Barack Obama is a long journey. But the presidency is still a comparatively small club—one that touches four different centuries—with just forty-three members. In the pages that follow, they request the pleasure of your company, and may you enjoy theirs, in turn.

GEORGE WASHINGTON
1732–1799

PRESIDENCY, 1789-1797

In the popular mind, George Washington is perceived more as noble warrior than as statesman: the heroic commander of the Continental Army, leading his troops across the cold, choppy Delaware River in Emanuel Leutze's famous painting. But Washington the president was every bit the giant that Washington the general was—shaping and defining the executive role on the fly, serving the country even before there was a city on the Potomac that would bear his name. (He was sworn in at Manhattan's Federal Hall and served his presidency there and in Philadelphia.)

With the same resourcefulness and calm that he used to motivate his ragtag troops during the Revolutionary War, Washington deftly held together a fledgling government riven by discord. Among the most contentious voices in his Cabinet were its two most prominent members: Alexander Hamilton, a proponent of strong federal power, and Thomas Jefferson, an advocate of states' rights. Washington, however, had little stomach for backroom rough-and-tumble. He hoped that the United States would not have political parties at all, arguing that "the common and continual mischiefs of the spirit of Party are sufficient to make it in the interest and the duty of a wise People to discourage and restrain it."

A bit too kumbaya for a revolutionary? Maybe. But while this vision proved naïve, such were his mediating skills that he guided his country and government through a period of deep philosophical schisms, making tough choices when he had to, such as endorsing Hamilton's idea of establishing a semi-public Bank of the United States over Jefferson's full-throated protest. He created the Cabinet system, asserted executive authority over foreign policy, set the two-term precedent, and kept his promise to visit all 13 former colonies. And in a feat not repeated by any president since, Washington even returned to active military duty, saddling up for battle in 1794, to help put down the Whiskey Rebellion, a short-lived revolt by some Pennsylvania farmers who were up in arms over a high federal excise tax on booze.

A reluctant president who had hoped to retire to his Virginia farm, Mount Vernon, after his first term expired, Washington was nevertheless the one man in America who conveyed the strength, decency, and might—he stood six feet two, weighed around two hundred pounds, and was, by all reports, physically imposing—to play the role of paterfamilias of what would prove to be a huge, dynamic, and unruly family.

—DAVID KAMP

1-Washington.

John Adams
1735–1826

PRESIDENCY, 1797–1801

John Adams was a rarity among U.S. presidents: a philosopher-statesman more than a politician. He was not by temperament a rebel (he loathed the French Revolution). And yet he became, paradoxically, one of the American Revolution's most important and consequential theorists: an impassioned writer and orator determined to forge a great nation out of a benighted colony.

Adams was the last man to doubt his own abilities: "Thanks to God," he wrote in his diary, "that [the Almighty] gave me stubbornness when I know I am right." Adams had the capacity, though, rare among the vain and gifted, to change his mind. Once convinced of the necessity of a full rupture from England, he devoted all his potent intellect to that goal. After the British closed the port of Boston following the famous Tea Party, it was Adams who helped draft the Declaration of Rights and Grievances, affirming colonists' rights to "life, liberty and property" on behalf of "free natural-born subjects." This was the theorist's equivalent of a shaken fist, and proved a conceptual cornerstone of the Declaration of Independence.

Adams had a passion for farming, law, politics, and, most of all, his highly intelligent wife, Abigail. To be sure, Abigail was often left alone with their five children (future president John Quincy among them) on their Massachusetts farm, while her husband went off to pursue his own ambitions. And she was, interestingly, an early advocate of a woman's right to divorce. But as First Lady she would prove to be a political partner and invaluable confidante not equaled until Eleanor Roosevelt.

After the Revolution, Adams's vaunted independence seemed to abandon him for a time. In 1789 he became vice president under Washington, toward whom he felt an unsuitable degree of deference. When Adams, a Federalist, argued in the Senate that his venerable boss should be addressed as "His Majesty the President," his suggestion provoked derision among fellow politicians, who dubbed the plump Adams "His Rotundity." Upon assuming the presidency himself, however, an Iron John emerged. Incensed when France demanded bribes as a condition of welcoming an American envoy, he rattled sabers before seeking a diplomatic solution. Next, he signed into law the Alien and Sedition Acts, making it a crime to publish "false, scandalous and malicious writing" about John Adams, or indeed any top government official. Much like certain provisions of the modern-day Patriot Act, this one had an expiration date— and fierce critics; within two years his successor would pardon everyone convicted.

"May none but honest and wise Men ever rule under this roof," wrote Adams in 1800, the first executive ensconced at what was then called the President's— later, the People's—House. (It was only in 1901 that the Executive Mansion was officially rechristened the White House.) Shortly after Adams's decree, his rival Thomas Jefferson took his place under that very roof.   —JUDY BACHRACH

2-J. Adams.

Thomas Jefferson
1743–1826

P R E S I D E N C Y , 1 8 0 1 – 1 8 0 9

He is the great conundrum of the American story: the Author of Liberty, who owned slaves. As shy and awkward in person as he was forceful with his pen, Thomas Jefferson two centuries ago retired the title of Presidential Polymath. Architect, horticulturist, inventor, natural scientist, viticulturist, political philosopher, he even published his own version of the New Testament, focusing on the words of Jesus and removing all references to miracles and divinity. Jefferson was the first president to serve both his terms in the new capital, at Washington, and the first to shake hands with the public. (His predecessors had merely deigned to bow.) Yet he considered the presidency the least of his achievements, omitting any reference to it on his tombstone, and—except for the Louisiana Purchase, which effectively doubled the size of the United States—he may have been right.

As principal author of the Declaration of Independence, he proclaimed truths that were then far from self-evident, and set the compass for the country that the British colonies would become. He sponsored the law in his home colony of Virginia requiring separation of church and state, which served as a model for the First Amendment. Before winning the presidency as the candidate of what would turn into the Democratic Party, he served first as minister to Paris in the run-up to the French Revolution (which he had misguidedly thought would be a bloodless triumph), then as George Washington's secretary of state and John Adams's vice president. He created (and designed the principal buildings of) the University of Virginia. His personal library became the basis of the modern Library of Congress after the British burned Washington in the War of 1812.

Tall and thin, with a shock of sandy hair in his youth, this most eloquent of men spoke with a lisp, so he preferred writing to talking. He sometimes greeted guests in homespun clothes and a pair of old bedroom slippers, but he had a taste for the finer things: on leaving the Executive Mansion, his wine bill topped $10,000.

His credo was succinct: "I have sworn upon the altar of God eternal hostility against every form of tyranny over the mind of man."

In the most intimate way, Thomas Jefferson embodied America's ambivalence about its original sin: there is strong evidence that he fathered several children by one of his favored slaves, Sally Hemings, but the balance of mutuality and mastery in their alliance may never be known. Like his old compatriot and competitor John Adams, he died on July 4, 1826, the fiftieth anniversary of the Declaration they drafted.

Adams, unaware that his friend had pre-deceased him by a matter of hours, would utter these prophetic last words: "Jefferson still survives." In truth, he still lives large, indeed.

—TODD S. PURDUM

3 - Jefferson.

— No 4 —

JAMES MADISON
1751-1836

PRESIDENCY, 1809-1817

Forever eclipsed in stature by his friend and predecessor, Thomas Jefferson— quite literally, given his reputed five-foot-two-inch height—Madison was never- theless a president of magnificent principle and fortitude. Taking the reins at a precarious moment in the young Republic's existence, when a still-hostile Brit- ain was seizing U.S. ships and trying to conscript American sailors into its navy against their will, he summoned the nerve to prompt Congress to declare war.

That Madison, of all presidents, should so boldly exercise his executive authority was a tribute to his ideological nimbleness—or, in his detractors' view, his willing- ness to flip-flop. Inherently wary of an overly powerful central government, Madi- son had earlier broken ranks with Alexander Hamilton, one of his Federalist Papers co-authors, to form, with Jefferson, what would become the first Republican Party (no relation to today's G.O.P.), which elevated the sovereignty of the states.

The War of 1812 was initially so unpopular in New England, where distrust of the Virginia-born president ran deep, that it kicked up talk of secession. But as momentum shifted in the United States' favor in key battles from the Great Lakes to New Orleans (this despite the redcoats' torching of the White House, in 1814), the American people were galvanized and Madison vindicated.

The president ceded the glamour quotient of the office to his vivacious wife, the former Dolley Payne Todd, who was the consummate Washington hostess, seventeen years his junior, and at least as many pounds heavier. Yet within Madi- son's tiny frame beat the heart of a canny, tenacious politician—and something of a sage. His central role in shaping the U.S. Constitution at the Philadelphia Convention of 1787 earned him the sobriquet "the Father of the Constitution." Madison modestly rejected this characterization, saying the document was "the work of many heads and many hands." But as the last of the original framers to actually serve as president, he was the Constitution's most forceful adherent and defender, all the way to the very end of his long life of eighty-five years.   —D.K.

4~ Madison.

JAMES MONROE
1758-1831

PRESIDENCY, 1817-1825

James Monroe, the son of wealthy Virginia planters, was the Zelig of America's founding years. In the iconic, if historically inaccurate, painting *Washington Crosses the Delaware,* Monroe appears as the staunch figure who holds the American flag, positioned just behind his commander. In real life, while serving under General George Washington at the Battle of Trenton, Monroe suffered a musket ball to the shoulder, which injured his axillary artery. He would eventually establish a plantation adjacent to Monticello, the estate of his confidant and mentor Thomas Jefferson. Monroe was also close to James Madison, Patrick Henry, Thomas Paine, John Quincy Adams, and Henry Clay (and was an enemy of Alexander Hamilton's). Prior to his two terms in office, Monroe served as Washington's minister to France, went head-to-head with Napoleon as the chief negotiator of the Louisiana Purchase during the Jefferson presidency, and became a key member of Madison's Cabinet. No gentleman slacker he.

Monroe began his career as a devoted member of Jefferson's Democratic-Republican Party, which stood opposed to Hamilton's notion of a strong federal government. But Monroe's experience in war and his knowledge of European intrigue led him to break with republican orthodoxy in arguing that volunteer state militias would not be enough to protect the expanding nation.

At first, while serving under Madison, he tried to tamp down hostilities between the U.S. and its former colonial masters. When that failed, he became an advocate for war and tried to establish a spy network to keep track of British movements, a gambit that Congress was not ready to approve. Lacking intelligence of the redcoats' progress at the outset of the War of 1812, Secretary of State Monroe did something that a Henry Kissinger, say, or a Hillary Clinton probably wouldn't have: he mounted his horse and led a cavalry patrol on a reconnoitering mission.

His presidency marked a time of expansion. He dealt ably with the delicate, Union-threatening prospect of Missouri's statehood and hashed out with Russia the parameters of what would become the Oregon Territory. On December 2, 1823, he laid out his muscular foreign-policy principles—later known as the Monroe Doctrine—in a speech that warned other countries to refrain from colonizing any independent nation in the Western Hemisphere, unless they meant to invite war with the United States. With these words Monroe asserted America's full independence and sense of itself as a power to be reckoned with on the world stage. In so doing, this security-minded president, in effect, completed the noble struggle he'd first joined as a scrappy eighteen-year-old volunteer under Washington.

—JIM WINDOLF

5~ Monroe.

JOHN QUINCY ADAMS
1767–1848

P R E S I D E N C Y ,   1 8 2 5 - 1 8 2 9

Was there ever a president as unfailingly earnest and cantankerous as John Quincy Adams? True, as secretary of state under James Monroe, Adams was responsible for the treaty with Spain that gave Florida to the United States. And true also, it was he, and not Monroe, who was the main author of the strident piece of bombast known as the Monroe Doctrine.

But it says something, surely, that even in 1790, when his famous father, John Adams, was vice president, Virginia-born John Quincy couldn't make a go of a career as a Boston lawyer: the fact that he loathed the very profession he had chosen didn't help matters. Despite such unpromising beginnings, family clout prevailed. In 1794, President George Washington appointed the younger Adams minister to the Netherlands; then, at the precise moment his dad became president, Adams was dispatched to Berlin—where he at last found his métier as a diplomat. While abroad, he also found London-born Louisa Catherine Johnson, a merchant's daughter, whom he decided to marry, even though she sang. (He detested the sound of women singing.) This was a brave decision, one made over the protests of then president Adams, who was averse to his son's taking on a foreign-born wife.

In 1824, when John Quincy Adams ran for president as a Republican, in a four-man race, he lost the preliminary balloting to Andrew Jackson. But on the second go-round, the choice of the nation's sixth president fell to the House of Representatives, which gave Adams the presidency. The outcome was largely attributable to the persuasiveness of a cunning Henry Clay, who, by way of thanks, was swiftly made secretary of state.

Jackson felt, as he told everyone, that he had been robbed of the presidency by an elitist. Four years later, Adams got the heave-ho, and Jackson got the nod. It was only then that Adams gained the kind of respect that had always eluded him. He went on to serve in Congress for seventeen years, becoming an eloquent opponent of slavery. He also resumed his legal practice, helping to represent the *Amistad* Africans before the Supreme Court, which ruled that his clients should not be returned to Spain as slaves. And it is to the Adams family that we are today beholden for the American precedent of father-son presidencies. —J.B.

6~ J. Q. Adams.

ANDREW JACKSON
1767–1845

PRESIDENCY, 1829-1837

It's one of the ironies of history that Andrew Jackson is perhaps best known as the face of the twenty-dollar bill, given that he despised paper currency. "Rag money," he called it. When he left the White House, after an eight-year run that strengthened the executive branch, he paid in gold for everything he purchased on the way back to his working plantation in Tennessee, the Hermitage.

Jackson may have been the most hotheaded man ever to hold the office. He fought two pistol duels. In the first, in 1788, both men escaped with their honor intact after deciding to fire into the air. The next time, Jackson, as part of an 1806 dispute about a horse-racing bet gone wrong, took a bullet in the chest. It broke two ribs and would remain lodged in his body for the rest of his life. Still on his feet, Jackson calmly fired at his opponent, killing Charles Dickinson, a well-to-do lawyer and farmer. Seven years later, Jackson took part in a wild gunfight in the heart of Nashville. He was shot in the arm in that scrap and, under a doctor's care, soaked two mattresses with blood. (Talk about trigger-happy. He married Rachel Donelson Robards before she was legally divorced—and the scandal of it, along with adultery talk, haunted them both.)

Violence seemed ingrained in Jackson. As a boy (he hailed from the South Carolina colony), this son of dirt-poor Scotch-Irish immigrants witnessed battlefield horrors while serving as a messenger in the Revolutionary War. He was wounded, captured by the British, and imprisoned. When the redcoats came back for more, in the War of 1812, Jackson was the general who led the decisive victory, at the Battle of New Orleans, for which he was celebrated as the savior of the Union. From there, he took on Indian tribes in what was then the Southwest. His soldiers called him "Old Hickory." Tribal chiefs dubbed him "Sharp Knife." Later the Spanish ceded Florida to the U.S. as a result of his seizing two of their forts during the first Seminole War.

Jackson was the first of seven presidents to be shot at by a lunatic gunman; his would-be assailant fired at close range but failed in his effort (soggy gunpowder). He was also the first to assemble a Kitchen Cabinet of trusted advisers. Although a slave owner, Jackson, a Democrat, used his status as commander in chief to threaten early South Carolina secessionists with military force. They caved. He was an iron-willed frontiersman who reasoned that, as president, he was the sole elected representative of all the American people. This Jacksonian notion of the office changed the job from mere prime minister and protector to something more fundamentally populist. No surprise, then, that toward the end of his second term he would become the first president to tour the country to adoring crowds.   —J.W.

7~Jackson.

MARTIN VAN BUREN
1782–1862

PRESIDENCY, 1837–1841

The first president born in the United States of America (and the first of non-British descent; his origins were Dutch), Martin Van Buren grew up listening to the politicians who stopped at his father's tavern in upstate New York, on their travels between Manhattan and Albany. To his credit, the impressionable Van Buren became a prodigious drinker known for never seeming the worse for wine.

Too poor to go to college, he studied law on his own, then climbed the political ladder, from county official to state senator, state attorney general to United States senator. A staunch Jeffersonian, nicknamed the Little Magician (he measured a mere five feet six inches), Van Buren helped build the political organization that would become the modern Democratic Party, and he served as Andrew Jackson's secretary of state and then vice president. He became the last sitting veep directly elected to the presidency until George H. W. Bush managed the same feat one hundred fifty-two years later. And just as Bush's single term was regarded as Ronald Reagan's third, so was Van Buren's presidency seen as a pale continuation of the effulgent Jackson's.

Elected only months before the Panic of 1837 plunged the country into the worst economic depression it had yet faced, Van Buren responded by holding fast to his principles of limited government and states' rights, but also moved to deposit federal funds in an independent treasury instead of counting on unreliable state banks. He opposed the annexation of Texas, knowing it would split his party over slavery. Van Buren's unsuccessful 1840 re-election campaign paid homage to his hometown of "Old" Kinderhook, New York, and helped popularize that most American of expressions: "O.K."   —T.S.P.

8 - Van Buren.

WILLIAM HENRY HARRISON
1773-1841

PRESIDENCY, 1841

William Henry Harrison had presidential cred. He was the son of the Revolutionary-era planter Benjamin Harrison V (whose signature appears on the Declaration of Independence, just below Jefferson's) and the grandfather of Benjamin Harrison, the twenty-third president. His ancestral Virginia home was located on a historically dicey spot: the Berkeley Plantation, tilled by more than a hundred slaves, and famously sacked by British troops led by Benedict Arnold. Some eighty years later, it would serve as headquarters for General George McClellan and his Union forces.

Back home after Berkeley's restoration, in 1784, young William met distinguished visitors such as Patrick Henry, Lafayette, and George Washington himself. At the age of eighteen, after returning from a year studying medicine in Richmond and Philadelphia, Harrison, upon his father's death, sold off his inherited lands and chose the hard path of a volunteer in the First U.S. Infantry. In a battle against Shawnee forces that included a young warrior named Tecumseh, Harrison impressed his superiors. Then, after eloping with a privileged East Coast girl, whose father did not want her marrying a soldier, he represented the Northwest Territory in Congress before President John Adams appointed him governor of the newly created Indiana Territory. On his gubernatorial watch, Harrison negotiated millions of acres away from the Indians and tried in vain to import slavery.

Harrison would confront Tecumseh twice more: first at the Battle of Tippecanoe, in Indiana, from which General Harrison emerged a hero, then during the War of 1812. In the latter clash, the British fled at the sight of Harrison's Northwest Army, but their Native American allies put up a fight. And after the U.S. victory in what would become known as the Battle of the Thames (in present-day Ontario), a mutilated corpse, reputedly Tecumseh's, lay still on the battlefield.

In 1840, the Whigs, in need of a presidential candidate, sent for the sixty-eight-year-old soldier, who had served as an Ohio congressman and senator before settling into retirement. Although Harrison was a polished pol from an old-line family, strategists presented him as a man of the people who dwelled in a log cabin and tippled hard cider. They sponsored parades, passed out stiff refreshments, and spread the slogans "Log Cabins and Hard Cider" and "Tippecanoe and Tyler Too." Soon, President Harrison stood coatless and hatless before a throng on a frigid morning in Washington, D.C. He delivered a whopper of an inaugural address, nearly two hours in length and rife with classical allusions. He caught a cold, which worsened, and he died thirty-two days later. —J.W.

9 - W. Harrison.

JOHN TYLER
1790–1862

P R E S I D E N C Y ,   1 8 4 1 – 1 8 4 5

John Tyler was known as "His Accidency" for having been the first man to assume the presidency due to his predecessor's passing. Because he was born into a prominent Virginia family, he considered himself a spiritual heir to the "Virginia Dynasty" presidents (Washington, Jefferson, Madison, Monroe), but never quite measured up to that vanguard.

Early in his political career, as a congressman and senator, he was a so-called Democratic-Republican, but he would eventually choose to quit the party when it was more or less taken over by Andrew Jackson, in whom Tyler detected "the spice of monarchy." In a marriage of convenience, Tyler, a firm states'-rights advocate, joined the federally minded Whigs.

Like Jackson, Tyler had served in the War of 1812. But unlike the tough-as-nails Hero of New Orleans, the patrician Tyler played only a brief, comic role in the conflict: awakened in a dorm room at the College of William and Mary by a report of oncoming British soldiers, Captain Tyler led his disheveled militia down a flight of stairs. Their haste caused a collision, and the men ended up in a pile. Then, upon reaching the supposed field of battle, they found not a single, solitary redcoat. Way to go, Ty.

The future president, an attorney, owned some seventy slaves, although he considered slavery "a dark cloud." When he found himself strapped for cash upon his election to the U.S. Senate, he sold a house slave named Ann Eliza to raise the funds sufficient for a Washington insider. Twice married, he was known to have fathered at least fifteen children.

After he was sworn in as William Henry Harrison's vice president, Tyler bolted from the inaugural ceremony and left town. A month later, messengers brought him the news of the president's death. Tyler traveled to the capital from his Virginia home—by horse, steamboat, and train—and immediately set about making what would be his greatest contribution to high office: while others argued that the Constitution was vague on whether the vice president should assume the chief executive's duties, Tyler asserted that he would serve not merely in an acting capacity but as the real deal. His interpretation stood. Soon enough, Tyler vetoed a bill put forth by his fellow Whigs. For that, he was tossed out of the party and made to face the first impeachment proceedings against a president, which failed. He went on to open diplomatic channels to China and oversee the annexation of Texas.

Upon leaving office, he was swept up in history's tide. In vain, Tyler worked to bring about a peaceful solution between North and South before joining the Confederates. He died a member of the Confederate House of Representatives, as the war between the states began to rage. He remains the only president not mourned in a state service.   —J.W.

10-Tyler·

JAMES KNOX POLK
1795-1849

PRESIDENCY, 1845-1849

He was the first dark horse to win the White House, and the last strong president before the Civil War, and if James K. Polk is not well known to the 21st-century public, historians admire him (as did Harry Truman) and consistently rank him with the greats or near greats among his peers. A divisive figure in his day, he bought Oregon and Washington from the reluctant British and went to war with Mexico for Texas and California—and won big, literally stretching the country from coast to coast.

A North Carolinian by birth and a Tennessee lawyer by vocation, Polk at age seventeen survived a brutal operation, with neither antiseptic nor anesthetic, to remove kidney (or gall-) stones. He was elected to the state legislature, made friends with Andrew Jackson, went to Congress, and served four years as Speaker of the House (the only one ever to win the presidency) before becoming governor of Tennessee and a viable Democratic vice-presidential candidate. In 1844, when the presumptive presidential nominees of both parties came out against the annexation of Texas, leaving room for an expansionist at the top of the ticket, Jackson backed a man committed to fulfilling the nation's Manifest Destiny, and Polk was nominated on the ninth ballot.

Humorless, arrogant, unforgiving, and fiercely partisan, Polk offered a succinct platform: lower the tariff, create an independent treasury to supplant corrupt private banks, acquire the Pacific Northwest, and take Texas and California. His predecessor John Tyler managed to annex Texas just days before Polk took office, but Polk could claim credit for all the rest.

Exhausted by his labors, he declined renomination, and died one hundred three days after leaving office, perhaps of the cholera he contracted on the long trip home to Nashville.

—T.S.P.

11-Polk.

ZACHARY TAYLOR
1784–1850

PRESIDENCY, 1849–1850

Zachary Taylor, who pastured his army horse, Old Whitey, on the White House lawn, was not our most formal president. He chewed and spit tobacco. He had a short neck; thick, untidy hair; and lips that stretched from cheek to cheek. His chest was so large and his legs so short that Taylor, horseman though he was, needed an orderly's boost to find his way into the saddle.

Dubbed "Old Rough and Ready" by his admirers—and there were plenty of those—Taylor was born in Virginia to a slave-owning planter family that maintained ten thousand acres in nearby Kentucky. At twenty-six, he married Margaret Mackall Smith, who came from prominent Maryland stock. Neither wealth nor privilege, however, appeared to soften him. From childhood, he wanted to be a soldier, and for most of his life he had a soldier's implacable approach to any issue. It was his view, for instance, that the best way to establish harmony between Native Americans and settlers was to maintain a strong American military. Call him a Homeland Security–firster.

After defeating the Seminoles at Lake Okeechobee, Taylor, then fifty-three, was made a brigadier general. In 1845, when the U.S. conferred statehood on Texas, a move that incensed Mexico and helped ignite the Mexican-American War, he and Old Whitey once again sprang into action. With only six thousand men he managed to defeat twenty thousand under the command of the Mexican general Santa Anna—at which point Taylor was regarded as prime presidential timber. (All in due course, however. Since the general had the miserly habit of refusing all postage-due letters, he didn't realize he'd been nominated for president until several days after the event.)

Once in office, Taylor maintained his stance as a firm, incorruptible independent. Although he had received the Whigs' nomination, for example, President Taylor pretty well ignored the party platform and enraged his backers by opposing protective tariffs. Southern plantation owners who had voted for him—having assumed he would share their views as a wealthy fellow slave owner—discovered too late that he was no fan of slavery's expansion into California or New Mexico, a hot-button issue at the time. Indeed, Taylor, ever forthright, warned would-be secessionists that they "would hang," just as he had "hanged deserters and spies in Mexico" in his soldier days.

Taylor never got to carry out his threat. In 1850, having served just sixteen months, the sixty-five-year-old president died of a curious gastrointestinal ailment (some say cholera)—to the last a self-contained, unpredictable curmudgeon, powered by pragmatism and fierce resolve.

—J.B.

12ᵗ Taylor.

— № 13 —

MILLARD FILLMORE
1800–1874

PRESIDENCY, 1850–1853

Unelected and never officially inaugurated, Millard Fillmore was a fill-in president in a fraught era. The running mate of a man he never even met until after the election of 1848—the much-loved Mexican-American War hero Zachary Taylor—Fillmore ascended to the presidency in July 1850, upon Taylor's demise. In so doing, he inherited not only a country fractured by the ongoing debate over slavery but the leadership of a Whig Party that was imploding over this very issue.

Fillmore was a self-made product of the hinterlands of upstate New York and therefore never knew slavery firsthand, as Taylor had. Yet he put the preservation of the Union above the abolition of slavery, deeming it "an existing evil" that northerners like himself would have to endure in order to prevent the South from seceding. The unwieldy slab of omnibus legislation that he pushed through Congress—the Compromise of 1850—reflected his conciliatory yet incoherent approach. Among other things, it admitted California to the Union as a free state but also introduced the Fugitive Slave Act, which dictated that runaway slaves would be returned to their owners by federal officers.

In Fillmore's defense, the Compromise prevented civil war from breaking out during his tenure. But to his many critics, Fillmore had merely papered over deepening rifts in the country and his own party (in which he was overshadowed by the elder and more charismatic figures Henry Clay and Daniel Webster). In 1852, the Whigs passed him over in favor of another much-loved Mexican-American War hero, Winfield Scott, who lost the national election to an obscure New Hampshire Democrat named Franklin Pierce. Thus were the Whigs effectively finished; Fillmore attempted a comeback in 1856 as the candidate of a disgruntled faction, the American Party (also known as the Know Nothings), but he was trounced, this time by James Buchanan. —D.K.

13-Fillmore.

— № 14 —

FRANKLIN PIERCE
1804-1869

PRESIDENCY, 1853-1857

His star-crossed life was straight out of one of the dark romantic tales of his friend Nathaniel Hawthorne. The son of a two-term governor of New Hampshire, Democrat Franklin Pierce had a precocious political career. Having been a state legislator before he turned thirty, he was elected to Congress, and served part of a term as senator. But he was a gossip and a drunk and was once arrested—while in office!—for running over an elderly woman with his horse. His marriage to Jane Means Appleton, a deeply religious temperance advocate, produced three sons, none of whom lived to adulthood and one of whom was nearly decapitated in front of their eyes in a railroad accident two months before Pierce assumed the presidency.

In a time of intensifying sectional strife, he was a weak and temporizing leader, who pressed for passage of the Kansas-Nebraska Act, which allowed residents of newly settled western territories to decide for themselves whether to allow slavery. Such polarizing edicts helped set the stage for the Civil War.

He was the first president to install a central heating system in the White House, and the first to have a Christmas tree there. Neither milestone was enough to save him from the ignominy of being spurned for a second term by his fellow Democrats, and on leaving office he declared: "There's nothing left . . . but to get drunk." (He has the distinction of being the only elected president ever denied renomination by his party.)

And we have Pierce to praise, or blame, for one delectable historical marker. His twentieth-century kinswoman Barbara Pierce became the wife of the first President Bush—and mother of the second.   —T.S.P.

14-Pierce.

JAMES BUCHANAN
1791–1868

PRESIDENCY, 1857–1861

The Nero of American presidents—ranked, from the day he left office, at or near the bottom of the bunch—James Buchanan fiddled as his country rushed headlong toward the Civil War. Stately, stuffy, stiff, he had a sterling career: member of Congress, minister to Russia, senator from Pennsylvania, secretary of state, minister to Great Britain. He ran unsuccessfully for president three times before finally winning in 1856, but his peerless résumé failed him in the job.

He naïvely believed he could forestall internecine conflict by keeping a sectional balance among his appointees. He often dithered, and when he acted, he invariably blundered, as he did by urging the admission of Kansas as a slave state, which angered many of his fellow Democrats and enraged the nascent Republican Party.

One of his eyes was nearsighted and the other farsighted, so he always cocked his head to the left, but nothing could compensate for his thorough lack of vision. He believed that southern states had no right to secede, but that the federal government had no authority to block them. He was the only president never to marry, and there is lively and not implausible speculation among modern historians that he may well have been gay: he lived for many years with a fellow bachelor, Senator William R. King of Alabama (Pierce's vice president).

When Buchanan surrendered the office to Abraham Lincoln, he declared: "If you are as happy in entering the White House as I shall feel on returning to Wheatland [his Pennsylvania farm], you are a happy man indeed."   —T.S.P.

15 - Buchanan.

16

ABRAHAM LINCOLN
1809-1865

PRESIDENCY, 1861-1865

He was the best writer ever to become president, so it should be no surprise that the essence of Abraham Lincoln has been best captured by poets, from his contemporary Walt Whitman to his fellow Illinoisan Carl Sandburg. "The facts and myths of his life are to be an American possession, shared widely over the world, for thousands of years," Sandburg once wrote, and only a poet could conjure a life so improbable, of such harsh privation and stunning achievement.

Lincoln served a single term in Congress, ran a failed campaign for the Senate, and just two years later won the White House, against a bevy of theoretically better men. He was mournful and melancholy, yet possessed of unquenchable humor. Self-taught, he was deeply learned in the majesties of the English language and the mysteries of human experience. A lawyer by trade and training, he was a storyteller by avocation, and he saw with epic clarity that it was his generation's task to make the nation live up to its founding creed.

As a Republican presidential candidate, this ungainly, even homely man was transformed by Mathew Brady's camera, appearing to voters as a figure of considerable stature. As a chief executive who valued wisdom over ego, he surrounded himself with a "team of rivals" to address the republic's perils. As an astute moral arbiter, he sought fairness in a merciless time.

He took office appealing to the "better angels" of the national character, but could not avoid a bloody civil war, which cost more than six hundred thousand lives—more than have been lost in all other American conflicts combined. He fought it first to save the Union—to make "the United States" a singular noun, an "is" and not an "are"—and then to free the slaves. In little more than two hundred seventy words at Gettysburg, he reaffirmed the power of the framers' vision, pledging a "new birth of freedom" for a nation that "shall not perish from the earth." His moral authority and foresight were such that his signing of the Emancipation Proclamation presaged the passage of the Thirteenth Amendment to the Constitution, in 1865, abolishing slavery in the United States.

His martyrdom, on Good Friday of that same year (he was felled by a bullet fired by the actor John Wilkes Booth, in Washington's Ford's Theatre), came barely five days after the end of the war and assured him a singular place in the hearts of the people. In 1909, on the centennial of his birth, he became the first American to be pictured on a United States coin—the penny, currency of the common man.

He was our tallest president (six feet four inches), and of the two score and three who have held the office he may well loom largest in history's eyes. His friend Edwin Stanton, his secretary of war, is said to have summed up Lincoln's standing just moments after his death: "Now he belongs to the ages." So he does.   —T.S.P.

16ᵗ Lincoln·

17

ANDREW JOHNSON
1808–1875

PRESIDENCY, 1865–1869

Long stigmatized as the only president ever to be impeached by the House of Representatives—that is, until Bill Clinton came along—Johnson exemplifies the dangers of tapping an underqualified vice-presidential candidate in the name of "balance." The nominal tapper in chief (though convention delegates, in truth, formally selected the running mate) was none other than Abraham Lincoln, who, in the 1864 election, selected Johnson because the latter was the only southern senator (born in North Carolina, he represented Tennessee) to continue to serve in the U.S. Senate even after his state had seceded from the Union.

As brave and admirable as Johnson's devotion to the Union was, he remained a pro-slavery Democrat, and when a bullet took Lincoln's life, Johnson, with just six weeks of executive experience, became, ironically, the president charged with overseeing the start of Reconstruction. Loathed on both sides—by his fellow southern Democrats as a pro-Union traitor and by the newly ascendant radical Republicans as a coddler of Confederates—Johnson spent his entire presidency in a state of bitter battle with various adversaries, culminating in a showdown with Congress over the newly passed Tenure of Office Act, which prohibited a president from removing a federal official without Senate approval. Calling Congress's bluff in 1868, Johnson fired his secretary of war, Edwin Stanton, prompting the House's vote to impeach him. Like Clinton one hundred thirty years later, Johnson was narrowly acquitted by the Senate—by a single nay—and therefore permitted to complete his term.

As ignominious a presidency as Johnson's was, his early life was yet another iteration of the classically American log-cabin trajectory: born to impoverished parents in North Carolina and barely literate until adulthood, he scrapped his way onto the political scene with his native intelligence and shrewd populist oratory. As he put it, "It's a damn poor mind that can only think of one way to spell a word." —D.K.

17-A. Johnson.

ULYSSES S. GRANT
1822–1885

PRESIDENCY, 1869–1877

Like George Washington before him, Grant was a war hero whom many in the political class regarded as the one man who could guide a fragile nation through parlous times. In 1868, as Andrew Johnson was winding down his disastrous tenure as the first Reconstruction president, Grant won the Republican nomination and easily defeated his Democratic opponent, Governor Horatio Seymour of New York.

But unfortunately, Grant, originally from Ohio, lacked Washington's political acuity. A brilliant battlefield tactician, he had shot up through the ranks during the Civil War, rising from mere colonel in 1861 to general-in-chief of all Union forces in 1864. Lincoln, his biggest booster, had held fast against Grant's doubters by proclaiming, "I can't spare this man—he fights."

As a president, though, Grant lacked fighting spirit. A naïf in a sea of Washington sharks, he appointed underqualified cronies and old army acquaintances to key positions, resulting in a series of corruption scandals that undermined his credibility and effectiveness. (His own private secretary, Orville Babcock, was implicated in a large-scale tax-fraud scheme known as the Whiskey Ring of 1875, an embarrassment that the loyal Grant exacerbated when he testified on Babcock's behalf, helping to secure a not-guilty verdict.)

Grant was somewhat more successful than Johnson in navigating between the desires of the wounded, combustible southern Democrats and the so-called radical Republicans, who favored the expansion of rights for freed slaves and punitive measures against ex-Confederates. During his tenure the Fifteenth Amendment was passed—guaranteeing male citizens of all races the right to vote—as was one of the nation's earliest civil-rights acts. But between his administration's corruption, the Democrats' renewed control of Congress in his second term, and the recession initiated by the stock-market panic of 1873, Grant finished out his presidency an impotent, compromised figure.

Posthumously, Grant eventually regained some of his pre-presidential esteem through his well-received memoirs, commissioned by Mark Twain in a successful effort to rescue the Grant family from penury and written against the clock as Grant was dying from throat cancer. He was entombed in a spectacular Beaux Arts–style mausoleum (popularly known as Grant's Tomb) that was sited in New York City's Riverside Park so that his widow, Julia, could easily visit from their retirement home upstate.   —D.K.

18-Grant.

RUTHERFORD BIRCHARD HAYES
1822–1893

PRESIDENCY, 1877–1881

At the age of thirty-nine, with prominent white streaks in his thick beard, Rutherford B. Hayes, a graduate of Kenyon College and Harvard Law, volunteered for a four-year stint in the Union forces when the Civil War broke out. A longtime opponent of slavery, he said he would rather be dead than do nothing to save the Union. After leaving behind a pregnant wife and three children in his Ohio home-town, he gained a reputation as "an intense and ferocious" warrior. He suffered five wounds, one severe, and rose from the rank of major to brevet major general.

His political career began while he was stationed in the Shenandoah Valley. Nominated for a congressional seat, Hayes refused to campaign, saying that "an officer fit for duty who at this crisis would abandon his post to electioneer for a seat in Congress ought to be scalped." Following one House term and three as governor of Ohio, he took the top spot on the Republican ticket in what would prove the most controversial and hotly contested presidential election in U.S. history (with the possible exception of George W. Bush versus Al Gore). New York Democrat Samuel Tilden led in popular votes by two hundred fifty thousand, but the Electoral College was too close to call. (Four states—three from the South—sent in two sets of electoral votes, clearly indicating lingering post–Civil War divisions.) The final decision fell to a committee of senators, congressmen, and Supreme Court justices, comprising eight Republicans and seven Democrats. When Hayes emerged victo-rious to take the presidency by a single electoral vote, enraged Democrats dubbed him "Rutherfraud." In fact, their party had cut a deal with the Republicans that it would not contest the election if the federal troops remaining in the South were withdrawn. Hayes complied, thus ending armed Reconstruction.

He was a steady, honest president who pledged to serve one term, and stuck to his word. He worked against nepotism and patronage in political appointments and used his veto power to weed out riders slipped into bills by southern Demo-crats hoping to weaken voting rights for African-Americans.

None other than Mark Twain praised the Hayes presidency for "its quiet & unostentatious, but real & substantial greatness," a remark echoed by subsequent historians. Following his White House years, Hayes worked to win federal subsi-dies for schools in poor districts and to lessen the plight of prisoners. He came to believe that the disparity in wealth between workers and their Gilded Age bosses was the country's greatest shame. Toward the end of his life, he summed up his go-slow progressivism by remarking, "I am a radical in thought (and principle) and a conservative in method (and conduct)." —J.W.

19-Hayes.

20

JAMES ABRAM GARFIELD
1831–1881

PRESIDENCY, 1881

The last of seven presidents to be born in a log cabin, and one of seven born in Ohio, James A. Garfield was the first left-handed president, and perhaps the poorest man ever to hold the office. He worked variously as a part-time teacher, a carpenter, a janitor, a professor of classics, and a lawyer.

His heroism in the Civil War propelled him to a seat in Congress, and he served nine terms before winning the Republican nomination for the presidency on the thirty-sixth ballot. He won office by just ten thousand votes, in the closest popular-vote margin then on record, and his mother became the first First Mom to attend her son's presidential inauguration.

Garfield fought against corruption in government, and had he lived longer he might well have pressed for civil-service reform. But just one hundred thirty-one days after being sworn in, he was shot by a disappointed office seeker, Charles Guiteau, in a Washington railroad station. Repeated efforts to find the bullet with non-sterile instruments led to severe infection and turned a wound that was originally three and a half inches long into a twenty-inch track that oozed pus. He died eighty days after the shooting, just shy of his fiftieth birthday.   —T.S.P.

20- Garfield.

21

CHESTER ALAN ARTHUR
1829–1886

PRESIDENCY, 1881–1885

Flashy of dress, suave of comportment, and possessed of the most outré facial-hair arrangement ever flaunted by a sitting American president (incredibly bushy sideburns that connected to a full mustache), Chester A. Arthur looked every bit the corrupt, high-living, tankard-swinging machine politician of the Gilded Age—which is precisely what many Americans feared they were getting when the man he served as vice president, James Garfield, succumbed to an assassin's bullet.

Yet Arthur turned out to be something of a pleasant surprise. Though a protégé of Roscoe Conkling, the wheeler-dealer New York senator and Republican Party boss—who had secured for Arthur the plum post of collector of the port of New York in 1871—Arthur became his own man as president. He eschewed Conkling-style political patronage and, indeed, expressly cracked down on it via the Civil Service Reform Act, which he signed into law in 1883. Conscious that his presidency was, to an extent, the result of an unseemly "spoils system"—his predecessor's killer had shot Garfield in anger over being denied an (irrationally) expected job in the new administration—Arthur was intent on reining in the de facto government policy of handing out jobs based on cronyism rather than qualifications.

Devotee of gracious living that he was, though, Arthur (born in Vermont, then raised a New York swell) couldn't resist allotting considerable time and government funds to the redecoration of the White House, which he felt had grown shabby. To this end, he commissioned Louis Comfort Tiffany, the stained-glass maestro, to serve as his interior decorator. (Arthur's wife, Nell, had died of pneumonia the year before he became president, thus depriving him of the traditional benefit of a First Lady's touch.)

It's possible that Arthur's casual defiance of conventional expectations was informed by his knowledge, kept secret from all but those closest to him, that he suffered from terminal kidney disease. No political opponent could deal him a blow worse than the one he knew was coming. Arthur died in November 1886, just twenty months after leaving office.   —D.K.

21-Arthur.

GROVER CLEVELAND
1837-1908

PRESIDENCY, 1885-1889; 1893-1897

One of the most endearing remarks to drop from any president's lips—"What is the use of being elected or re-elected unless you stand for something?"—was uttered by the historically neglected Grover Cleveland. He had never intended to become a politician (until 1881, he was a contented New Jersey–born bachelor practicing law in Buffalo), and in some ways the plainspoken executive never wholly succeeded.

In his time, the portly Cleveland was known, with reason, as the "Guardian President." His honesty and candor appealed to the middle class, as did his admirable opposition to the temperance movement. But his campaign for the highest office was very nearly derailed. In July 1884, under the headline A TERRIBLE TALE, the *Buffalo Evening Telegraph* breathlessly revealed that Cleveland, years earlier, had fathered a son out of wedlock. Republicans massing at campaign stops greeted the Democratic presidential candidate with "Ma, Ma—where's my pa?" Cleveland, although always uncertain about the matter, decided to accept paternity, and won by a very narrow margin.

The first four years in the White House proved a source of great joy to its occupant. Callers and visitors were delighted to find that, on occasion, it was the president himself who answered the White House phone—and the front door. In 1886, Cleveland married pretty twenty-one-year-old Frances Folsom in the Blue Room; in fact, he is the only president to have tied the knot while in office. (The couple's eldest child, for whom the candy bar Baby Ruth was named, died tragically at age twelve.) When Cleveland, a rare Democrat in a string of Republican presidents, lost in his 1888 bid for re-election, Frances cautioned a White House servant as they packed up the place: "Take good care of all the furniture and ornaments in the house, for I want to find everything just as it is when we come back again." Her words proved prophetic. Cleveland's Republican rival, Benjamin Harrison, lasted just one term.

Cleveland's second national victory, which remains unique in American annals for being non-consecutive, was jammed with activity. Right after he assumed office, the Panic of 1893 socked the stock market, a crisis intensified by a severe gold shortage. Economic depression ensued. He sent federal troops to crush a railroad strike. And when Great Britain sparred with Venezuela over boundary issues, Cleveland expanded the way the Monroe Doctrine's dictates were interpreted, establishing American dominion over disputes within the hemisphere. But his firmness and resolve had their downsides. The Democrats, considering him too resistant to the Populist movement, washed their hands of him and, in 1896, nominated the celebrated William Jennings Bryan. Cleveland would decline all further pleas to run. His last words, after he suffered a heart attack, in 1908: "I have tried so hard to do right."   —J.B.

22·24 - Cleveland·

BENJAMIN HARRISON
1833-1901

PRESIDENCY, 1889-1893

Described (accurately) as "little, gray, and cold," with a handshake "like a wilted petunia," Benjamin Harrison, all five feet six inches of him, won the 1888 presidential election the old-fashioned way: through the Electoral College. His Democratic rival, Grover Cleveland, was actually more popular—by more than one hundred thousand votes. Naturally, Harrison ascribed his victory to "Providence."

He would have been more forthright had he ascribed it to genealogy: Harrison was the grandson of William Henry Harrison, the ninth American president. Because he grew up on a North Bend, Ohio, farm close to his venerable grandfather, young Benjamin was certain he was destined to have a remarkable life.

This actually never quite happened. True, Harrison launched his career by generally supporting the winning side: he worked for Abraham Lincoln in 1860, and rose to the rank of brigadier general during the Civil War. But his ambition had its limits. He passed up the chance to run for an Indiana congressional seat and twice rebuffed state Republicans' efforts to name him their candidate for governor. As fate would have it, the party's nominee in 1876, Congressman Godlove Orth, had to withdraw in a financial scandal. And Harrison, upon returning home from a family trip to the Great Lakes, found surging crowds at the railroad station: he'd been nominated without his knowledge or consent. After all that, he lost narrowly (though he rebounded and served one term in the Senate).

It didn't escape notice that Harrison was ill at ease in public, his hands so badly afflicted with dermatitis that he always had to wear gloves. Despite such drawbacks, he was a man of strong convictions, with fierce populist instincts that were often at odds with those of his own party. "I pity the man who wants a coat so cheap that the man or woman who produces the cloth will starve in the process," he once said.

As president, he supported high tariffs to protect American companies, endorsed bills to prevent the South from denying the vote to black Americans, tried to annex Hawaii, and spearheaded an effort to create massive forest reserves in the American West. None of this brought him the popularity he desired: indeed, those stiff surcharges likely helped lead to a depression that eventually flattened the U.S. economy. In 1892, there was relief all around when Cleveland finally swept into office. Harrison, defeated but exhilarated, told his family he felt like he'd been freed from prison.   —J.B.

23-B·Harrison·

— № 25 —

WILLIAM MCKINLEY
1843–1901

PRESIDENCY, 1897–1901

Because the irrepressible Teddy Roosevelt once described William McKinley as having "no more backbone than a chocolate éclair," the nation's twenty-fifth president was long perceived as a mediocre leader. At best. The Ohio-born Republican—often in the thrall of unappetizing cronies from his days as a congressman, then as Buckeye State governor—was forever vacillating.

But in recent years, a fonder assessment of McKinley has surfaced. The impetuous Roosevelt had delivered that éclair analogy a month after Spain was accused (without a scintilla of evidence) of blowing up the U.S. battleship *Maine*, which he felt demanded vengeance. In Roosevelt's corner was William Randolph Hearst, whose newspapers wielded the kind of power their modern-day counterparts will never attain. "Remember the *Maine*—to Hell with Spain" became the battle cry of American xenophobes who thought the best way of punishing the supposed enemy was to wrest away control of Spain's prized colony, Cuba.

On April 25, 1898, Congress declared war. Within three short months McKinley, almost despite himself, became the beneficiary of the legislators' rage. The young nation was carried away by new, expansionist appetites and a determination to control its own hemisphere. What Secretary of State John Hay would call a "splendid little war" resulted in Spain's granting Cuba independence—a short-lived gift, as it swiftly became a U.S. protectorate. Guam, the Philippines, and Puerto Rico, all once Spanish as well, also fell under American control.

Somehow this overnight transformation of a country appears to have altered McKinley. To help crush the Boxer Rebellion, he sent two thousand troops to China. Determined to protect U.S. property rights in Nicaragua, he twice intervened there. "President of the money kings and trust magnates," the anarchist Emma Goldman dubbed the man who would put America on an imperialist footing.

On September 6, 1901, on a visit to Buffalo, New York, McKinley was warned by his secretary to skip a reception in his honor. "Why should I? No one would wish to hurt me," the president replied. Among those anxious to shake his hand was Leon Czolgosz, an unemployed factory worker who was a follower of Goldman's. Czolgosz extended a hand swathed in a handkerchief that concealed a gun. He shot McKinley twice—the second bullet hit the victim's kidney and pancreas. McKinley lingered for eight days, weak with gangrene and impatient for death. "It is useless, gentlemen," he told his doctors. "I think we ought to have a prayer."   —J.B.

25- McKinley.

THEODORE ROOSEVELT
1858-1919

PRESIDENCY, 1901-1909

T.R., as he was called, had a bloodlust, hunting big game from the Amazon to the Nile. He was a marksman and, though a volunteer, the pride of the U.S. Cavalry, gaining early fame as a Rough Rider at the helm of the 1898 assault on San Juan Hill, in Cuba, during the Spanish-American War. He would become America's youngest president ever, assuming office at age forty-two—nine months after vacating the New York governor's mansion—following the assassination of fellow Republican William McKinley. Roosevelt himself, while campaigning in 1912, was shot at point-blank range by an unstable tavern owner. T.R. recovered, remarking, "It will take more than that to kill a bull moose!," thus christening his short-lived Bull Moose Party.

Theodore Roosevelt (fifth cousin of F.D.R.) was a child of means, raised in Manhattan and Long Island's Oyster Bay, whose father had helped found the American Museum of Natural History. He was a Harvard-educated intellect, naturalist, and writer—the first president to publish a book while in office (he contributed a piece about deer to a wilderness anthology). He was worldly despite having spent long stretches during his twenties on a Badlands ranch, where, in 1884, he had sought refuge and solace after the death of his mother *and* his first wife within hours of each other. He had a bearish presence, galloping enthusiasm, and a radiant, toothy smile which so enamored the populace that the teddy bear was named in his honor.

From the instant he barreled into the Oval Office, T.R. expanded the executive branch, asserting his political mojo by taking on Congress, the railroads, and union bosses; issuing presidential edicts; and charging forty-four corporations with antitrust violations—all in the name of extracting for the average workingman a "square deal." He supported women's suffrage and laid the early lattice of a social safety net, from welfare measures to workplace improvements to a nascent consumer-protection agency. And even though Roosevelt was a colonialist in his racial views, he invited educator-activist Booker T. Washington to break bread at the White House.

On the international stage the president brokered the building of the Panama Canal, ramped up the navy, and interceded to end the Russo-Japanese War, collecting a Nobel Peace Prize to go with his elk and rhino heads. But it was on the American outdoors that he left his most significant mark. In all, he would set aside two hundred thirty million acres of wilderness for preservation—roughly the equivalent of all the real estate from Maine to Georgia. "I don't think any President ever enjoyed himself more than I did," Teddy said in 1910, having bid Washington adieu to stalk elephants and wildebeests in East Africa. "Moreover, I don't think any ex-President ever enjoyed himself more." —DAVID FRIEND

26~J·R~

WILLIAM HOWARD TAFT
1857–1930

PRESIDENCY, 1909–1913

William Howard Taft was an intelligent, sweet-natured man who hated being president. He was a plodder who liked to examine all sides of an issue before limping to a decision. He also had a sensitive side that left him out of step with his alpha-male peers. He couldn't recall the names of key supporters and abhorred the jabs of journalists, who made sport of his mountainous physical form and his tendency to shirk the duties of his office. "Please Mr. President," cried *The New York Times.* "Do something!"

Despite his rise to the highest office in the land, Taft was a judge at heart. At thirty-four, he had worked on the federal bench in his home state of Ohio and had loved it. As he ascended through the Republican ranks, appointed to various posts by William McKinley and Theodore Roosevelt, he nursed a secret hope: to return to the bench someday as a Supreme Court justice. But his ambitious, domineering wife and his best friend in Washington, the equally ambitious and domineering Roosevelt (who remarked that Taft possessed "the most lovable personality I have ever come in contact with"), had other designs for him. Taft was an admittedly ambivalent nominee on the 1908 Republican ticket: as a matter of principle, he was wary of the Progressive Movement's prescription for using the executive branch to advance social reform. Yet Taft sailed to victory on the canny strategies of his White House predecessor.

From the moment he occupied the Oval Office, work began to accumulate on Taft's desk. And even though he racked up notable achievements in the areas of conservation and anti-trust policy, he understood that a president needed his downtime. He took unaccompanied strolls through Washington, played leisurely rounds of afternoon golf, rode in the first presidential automobile, made excursions to nearby department stores, and went on long train journeys to deliver a dull speech and have a big meal at a state fair far from the job he loathed.

In his one term as president, he took solace in food—a twelve-ounce steak, oranges, and buttered toast for breakfast, with coffee and cream; nine-course extravaganzas for his dinner. His weight ballooned from two hundred eighty-seven pounds to three hundred fifty-five, and he developed gout. At Cabinet meetings he fell into deep slumbers. An aide had to punch him or cough loudly to wake him. And the mishaps! When Taft got stuck in the White House bathtub, it took several aides to pull him out. In New York City, a trolley smashed into an auto carrying the hapless leader down Eighth Avenue.

In 1921, at last, President Warren G. Harding appointed him chief justice of the Supreme Court. Taft held the job, happily and a hundred pounds lighter, until a month before his death, in 1930.   —J.W.

27-Taft.

WOODROW WILSON
1856–1924

PRESIDENCY, 1913–1921

Woodrow Wilson, who led the nation into World War I reluctantly, had loathed war since childhood. Though born in Virginia, he was raised in Augusta, Georgia, and during the Civil War he watched Yankee forces march on the city. His next home—Columbia, South Carolina—was burned to the ground by drunken soldiers.

Trauma somehow honed his abilities, his ideals, and his determination to leave his southern roots behind. By age forty-six he was president of Princeton University. Eight years later he became the Democratic governor of New Jersey. His accomplishments: campaign-finance reform and a primary law that allowed voters—not party bosses—to nominate candidates.

In 1912 he aimed for the presidency in a move notable for its timing: Theodore Roosevelt walked out of the Republican convention that year, splitting his party's vote. Wilson then took the White House with only forty-two percent of the popular tally.

His reputation as a progressive was hard-earned: Wilson was a staunch union backer who promoted tariff reductions and curbs on big business. It's thanks to him that in 1913 the Federal Reserve was created, and worth noting that he intended the Fed to actually regulate banks. Although earnest in his convictions—Wilson's re-election campaign slogan during the early years of World War I was "He Kept Us out of War"—by 1917 even he recognized that American neutrality was at an end. Not only had the Germans sunk the luxury liner *Lusitania,* but a German plot to ally itself with Mexico was uncovered. "It is a fearful thing to lead this great peaceful people into war," he acknowledged, "but the right is more precious than peace." By "right" he meant the imperative to make the world safe for democracy.

Woodrow Wilson's dream of greater global harmony never left him. In 1918, five months before the Allies' triumph in the Great War, he laid out his plans for a League of Nations, which the U.S. Senate twice rejected. It was a notion that epitomized the Wilsonian ideal: an organization devoted to ensuring universal human rights, achieving disarmament, and bringing together fractious nations to hash out their differences rather than resort to bloodshed. Within a year, Wilson received the Nobel Peace Prize and the League became a reality as an initial forty-five nations signed on.

The League, more to the point, became the forerunner of the United Nations, founded in 1945, which this dreamer never lived to see. "Some people call me an idealist—well, that is the way I know I am an American," Wilson said, shortly before a stroke would silence him. —J.B.

28-Wilson

— № 29 —

WARREN GAMALIEL HARDING
1865–1923

P R E S I D E N C Y ,   1 9 2 1 – 1 9 2 3

What can we say about a man whom many historians rank as among the very worst presidents in American history? Just this: unlike some of the runners-up we've elected, Republican Warren G. Harding had the grace to acknowledge from the outset that he was in over his head.

He was absolutely right. Although Harding had his strong suits—twice-weekly poker games, and a fondness for whiskey, golf, and chasing women—his judgment was not infallible. His closest associates while he was in the White House were a bunch of crooks known as "the Ohio Gang," after the state of Harding's birth. It was they who persuaded Harding to appoint Albert B. Fall as secretary of the interior—an embarrassing selection, especially when word got out that Fall, soon after taking the post, had received gifts from oil magnates worth $404,000 (about $4 million today); the entrepreneurs, in turn, got leases on petroleum-rich public land. This error of judgment became known as the Teapot Dome Scandal, and it provoked a long series of criminal and civil suits, along with an innovative Supreme Court decision, which established Congress's right to compel testimony.

No one ever proved exactly that Harding was a crook. But his affections were at least as imprudent and public as his Cabinet choices: Carrie Phillips, a German sympathizer during World War I, actually blackmailed the president while he was in office (the Republican Party generously paid her off); Nan Britton, a dashing blonde thirty years his junior, visited him regularly in—where else?—the Oval Office.

In 1923, at the age of fifty-two, Harding became violently ill with what some claimed was food poisoning. Others maintained, however, that his wife, Flossie, had poisoned him in order to save the office of the presidency from further embarrassment. As it turned out, Harding died, after two years and five months in office, of a heart attack.   —J.B.

29-Harding.

30

CALVIN COOLIDGE
1872–1933

PRESIDENCY, 1923-1929

It's appropriate, in hindsight, that the Jazz Age—a cocktail shaker of motor-cars and radio, the Babe and the Lindy Hop, Scott and Zelda, Al Jolson and the talkies—was presided over by a dour Puritan of few words who came to be known as Silent Cal. "During six years of America's high-living, hard-drinking, loose-moraled, money-making postwar holiday spree," observed *Vanity Fair*'s Paul Gallico, "the nation was governed |by| a man of unimpeachable honesty, selfless courage, and practically nonexisting speech.... While all of us were losing our heads slightly in one way or another, he was keeping his."

The son of a popular Vermont civil servant, Calvin Coolidge had an ingrained New England reticence, reinforced by the loss of his mother and sister during his youth, and honed at idyllic Amherst College. A lawyer elected to a string of public posts, stay-the-course Coolidge was snapped up as Harding's running mate after taking a stern stand, as Massachusetts governor, against union intransigence in the Boston Police Strike of 1919. When the smoke cleared following Harding's scandals—and his sudden death in office, in 1923—Coolidge was the last moralist standing.

Frugal, isolationist, eat-your-greens Cal (who would be elected to his first full term under the banner "Keep Cool with Coolidge") was at the tiller for most of the 1920s, a period of vertiginous prosperity for many Americans. Although the president was painfully tight-lipped in person (when a female dinner guest boldly told him she'd bet a friend she could coax three words out of him, he reportedly replied, simply, "You lose"), he embraced the new powers of mass media by holding forth on the radio, at press conferences, and in a flurry of public appearances at which he had a propensity for cultural cross-dressing, frequently adorned in ranch-hand duds or Native American regalia.

Along with his Treasury secretary, financier Andrew Mellon, Coolidge resisted granting aid to needy farmers and urged tax cuts for the wealthy, as Republican presidents are wont to do. (Unsurprisingly, during the propulsive 80s, Ronald Reagan would use Coolidge as one of his models.) On the president's watch, stock speculators ran fast and loose, setting off the Crash of '29. But Coolidge evaded the catastrophe by deciding not to run for a second term—fleeing D.C. seven months before the roof fell in.

And could anyone have concocted a more bland post-presidency? In 1929, Coolidge, naturally, became president of the American Antiquarian Society—and director of the New York Life Insurance Company—before dying of a heart attack in 1933. When informed of his passing, the onetime *Vanity Fair* writer and Algonquin wit Dorothy Parker remarked, "How can they tell?" —D.F.

30~Coolidge·

31

HERBERT CLARK HOOVER
1874-1964

PRESIDENCY, 1929-1933

With seemingly twice the combined brainpower of his two predecessors, the dunderheaded Warren Harding and the phlegmatic Calvin Coolidge—both of whom he served as secretary of commerce—Herbert Hoover appeared poised to advance the United States toward, in his words, "the final triumph over poverty." While it was the Republican National Committee, rather than the candidate himself, that had audaciously promised "a chicken in every pot" during the 1928 campaign, the Iowa-born Hoover seemed to have the right stuff for greatness. Orphaned at nine, he willed himself into the first graduating class of Stanford University, amassed a seven-figure fortune as a mining engineer and consultant by the time he'd turned forty, and became distinguished for his public-service works, spearheading food-relief efforts during and after World War I.

That he is now seen as the embodiment of governmental callousness and in-effectuality—his name forever attached to the "Hooverville" shantytowns that arose in the early years of the Great Depression—is not entirely fair. Neither he nor his Democratic opponent, Al Smith, could have foreseen the stock-market crash of 1929, which happened just seven months into Hoover's term. Nor did he sit idly by as the financial crisis worsened. In the spring of 1929 he called a special session of Congress to address the grim state of American agriculture, which had darkened the fields of the Republic for the previous decade. In 1932, in defiance of his long-held laissez-faire approach to economic policy, he established the Reconstruction Finance Corporation (R.F.C.), a sort of proto–New Deal government agency that offered loans and aid to banks, businesses, and state and local governments.

But to the American public, this was way too little, way too late; Hoover's reluctance to take bolder, more interventionist steps to right the economy set the stage for Franklin Delano Roosevelt's landslide victory in '32 and the real, unfettered New Deal (which, it must be said, expanded upon Hoover's R.F.C.). Bitter but unbroken, Hoover went on to have the longest afterlife of any ex-president, living to 1964 (he died at age ninety) and rehabilitating his image somewhat by serving on government-efficiency commissions at the behest of Presidents Harry Truman and Dwight Eisenhower.

—D.K.

31-Hoover.

FRANKLIN DELANO ROOSEVELT
1882–1945

PRESIDENCY, 1933–1945

He was a son of the aristocracy, related by blood or marriage to eleven former presidents and bred to have no ambition grander than to be a country squire. Yet Franklin Delano Roosevelt, born in Hyde Park, New York, defied that Wasp stereotype to become an American archetype: the man who persuaded a desperate nation that it had nothing to fear but fear itself.

Meeting him, his friend Winston Churchill once said, was like opening your first bottle of champagne. Jaunty, haughty, charming, clever, forthright, indirect, he betrayed his wife, Eleanor (who would later seek companionship and emotional support from journalist Lorena Hickok), by having an affair with Eleanor's social secretary, then contracted polio at age thirty-nine and never again walked unaided. He emerged from that ordeal with deeper reservoirs of character. With Eleanor as partner and prod, he became the Democratic governor of New York and then president during the depths of the Great Depression. Through swift action—described in homey metaphors in "fireside chats" on the radio—Roosevelt unleashed his upper-class accent and supreme self-assurance to bolster the courage of a shaken country.

His New Deal deployed government money to build great public works, and the presidency's psychological power to restore public confidence. He created post offices and roads, hydroelectric dams and theaters, and he carved out parkways and pleasure grounds from great stretches of the American wilderness. He reduced risk and provided security for vast sectors of society—the unemployed, the banks, home lending, labor, corporations—helping make the business world less of a crapshoot than it had been since the dawn of the Industrial Revolution. If there is historical debate about the economic utility of some of his policies, there is little doubt about the psychological benefits: he gave the workingman his pride back and the elderly their dignity through his jobs programs and Social Security. He saved capitalism from itself.

Roosevelt prepared a reluctant populace and resistant Congress for the coming of the Second World War, and used the same force of personality that he applied to domestic politics to wage it for nearly three and a half years. Together with those uneasy allies, Churchill and Stalin, he pioneered the statecraft of summitry and bridged a world that was growing smaller by the day. If he could not walk himself, he nevertheless led his nation on a great march to the future.

Elected four times (twice as many as any other president), he died on the very eve of victory. In his last speech, drafted for delivery but never uttered, he wrote: "The only limit to our realization of tomorrow will be our doubts of today. Let us move forward with strong and active faith."   —T.S.P.

32-F·D·R·

33

HARRY S. TRUMAN
1884-1972

PRESIDENCY, 1945-1953

"I felt like the moon, the stars and all the planets had fallen on me," he said of April 12, 1945, the day F.D.R. died and Harry Truman became a wartime commander in chief—after just eighty-two days of being resolutely ignored as vice president. The man was playing poker when the news broke. And yet Truman, unseasoned though he was, proved an extraordinary, Everyman leader who was perhaps never enough appreciated while he was still alive. Firm, decisive, and willing to make the kind of instinctive, tough decisions for which he acknowledged responsibility, he understood the necessity of resolve. THE BUCK STOPS HERE, a sign first posted by a warden in an Oklahoma reformatory, had pride of place on Truman's Oval Office desk.

Truman's origins weren't auspicious: he had spent twelve unhappy years as a farmer in Independence, Missouri, and a few more as an unsuccessful haberdasher. He was friendly with a low-life Democratic boss who had first made Truman a judge and then helped him become a senator. Small wonder he had been briefed on little as vice president—least of all the atomic bomb. It was the deployment of this weapon that would prove the most controversial decision of his presidency—albeit one that has forever been weighed against the sizable potential loss of American life had it not been used. (The conventional wisdom in 1945 was that without it an Allied victory might have required another full year of war.) He ordered the new bombs dropped on Hiroshima and Nagasaki on August 6 and 9: more than one hundred thousand Japanese civilians were instantly killed, and in years to come at least that many more would die from the lingering effects of radiation exposure.

Truman faced a postwar avalanche of crises: a Soviet-controlled Eastern Europe; a pro-Soviet China; a Cold War; at home, high inflation and a divided Democratic Party. In the 1948 election, he eked out a slim margin of victory (to almost everyone's amazement) against New York governor Thomas Dewey. But even this triumph was short-lived. By 1950, Republican senator Joseph McCarthy was accusing the administration of being "soft on Communism." At the same time, Communist North Korea invaded South Korea, and once again Truman led the nation in war, although cautiously. Complicating matters was General Douglas MacArthur, a valiant, immensely popular, yet trigger-happy commander. Truman, never one to sidestep a controversial decision, fired him.

In 1953, Truman refused to run for re-election and returned, aptly, to Independence. He had observed early on, with his usual bluntness, that a president was nothing more than "a glorified public relations man who spends his time flattering, kissing and kicking people to get them to do what they are supposed to do anyway." He never altered that view.   —J.B.

33-Truman·

34

DWIGHT DAVID EISENHOWER
1890-1969

PRESIDENCY, 1953-1961

'I am greatly disturbed," Winston Churchill told a friend soon after Dwight D. Eisenhower was elected president. "I think this makes war so much more probable." In fact, the opposite proved true. Eisenhower, the supreme commander of the Allied forces in Europe in World War II, called war "the saddest of all human activities." While serving as the nation's first five-star general, he quietly opposed the atomic assault on Japan. And the first thing he did, upon replacing Truman in the White House, was to end U.S. involvement in Korea, which he considered a quagmire.

Eisenhower presided over a peaceful time in American history. His detractors would say that it was *too* peaceful and that he was the perfect match for a national mood of numbing conformity. This was a man, after all, who installed a putting green on the White House lawn and enjoyed TV dinners with his wife, Mamie. But Eisenhower's chief interest was in maintaining the calm after the storm of war.

The first hero president since Ulysses S. Grant, Eisenhower, the son of pacifist Mennonites, was a mild Republican. He favored cooperation with European and Soviet leaders at a time when the isolationist wing of his party, led by Joseph McCarthy, was obsessed with rooting out supposed subversives on American soil. The 1952 campaign slogan "I Like Ike," based on an Irving Berlin lyric, wasn't a meaningless rhyme. Eisenhower had earned his stars, in part, because of his knack for creating something like consensus among the outsize characters who had a hand in running the war's European theater—Roosevelt, Churchill, Stalin, de Gaulle, Montgomery, Marshall, and Patton. During two popular terms, Ike left a lasting domestic mark as well: appointing the socially progressive Earl Warren as chief justice of the Supreme Court, shepherding the Interstate Highway System (the most extensive national public-works project ever), and upholding constitutional law—even though he clearly favored segregation—which effectively set in motion the racial integration of American schools.

As president, this unassuming man from Abilene, Kansas (though born in Denison, Texas), got few points for style. He lacked the blueblood charm of his old boss Roosevelt; possessed little of the common-man folksiness of his predecessor, Truman; and had not one whit of the panache of his successor, John F. Kennedy. But Ike was, in the end, the real thing.

—J.W.

34 - Eisenhower.

— № 35 —

JOHN FITZGERALD KENNEDY
1917–1963

PRESIDENCY, 1961-1963

He was a child of privilege, born to a power-smitten Massachusetts political family. He attended Choate and Harvard, vacationed in Palm Beach, Cape Cod, and the Riviera, and received a million dollars from his father upon turning twenty-one. But he had been sickly as a boy, beset by measles, scarlet fever, and whooping cough, and later he had three conditions that would prove chronic—colitis, Addison's disease, and an unstable back. Partly as a defense mechanism, partly out of breeding and temperament, he developed a vivacious manner and quick wit.

In 1941, after failing army and navy physicals, young Jack prevailed upon his well-connected father, Joe Kennedy Sr., to pull strings to get him into the service. During a patrol gone wrong in the Pacific, a Japanese destroyer rammed PT 109, the torpedo boat commanded by Lieutenant Kennedy, slicing it in half. The survivors clung to the hull for nine hours, until he led a five-hour swim to a deserted island.

After serving in the House and Senate, Kennedy, while running for president, again found reason to hide his poor health, not to mention the regimen of amphetamines and steroids that kept him going. (In a media environment more decorous than our own, he had little trouble concealing his extramarital affairs and his ties to shady associates.) The Democrat defeated Richard Nixon by a narrow margin in the popular vote, becoming the first Roman Catholic to sit in the Oval Office and, at age forty-three, the youngest man to be elected president. In his elegant, inspiring inaugural address, he instructed his fellow citizens, "Ask not what your country can do for you; ask what you can do for your country."

With movie-star looks (and movie-star pals), J.F.K. charmed the media and home-viewing audience, holding weekly televised press conferences. Against the backdrop of Cold War intensity, he appeared cool and glamorous, an image enhanced by his wife, Jacqueline, possibly the most chic and fetching of all First Ladies. Bolstered by incredibly young and bright, if relatively inexperienced, aides—including brother Robert, his attorney general—Kennedy issued executive orders to combat discrimination against African-Americans, established the Peace Corps, set a course for the moon, and stepped up the U.S. presence in Vietnam. And, yes, the crises. After sponsoring the ill-fated Bay of Pigs invasion, undertaken by Cuban exiles against Fidel Castro, Kennedy found himself on the brink of an apocalyptic war with the Soviet Union. Even so, the president's reputation soared after staring down Russia's Nikita Khrushchev in his attempt to deliver nuclear missiles to Cuba.

At the time of his assassination, in Dallas, on November 22, 1963, it seemed as if his presidency was just beginning. What followed, instead, was a period of sorrow and paralysis, then deep reflection, then division, and over the ensuing decade the country would recast its priorities socially, culturally, and militarily.   —J.W.

35-Kennedy.

36

LYNDON BAINES JOHNSON
1908–1973

PRESIDENCY, 1963-1969

A salty son of the Texas Hill Country and a classic Washington insider; a bare-knuckled backroom operator and a compassionate champion of the poor; a notorious womanizer and a husband dedicated to his sweetheart, Lady Bird; a divisive war president and the Democratic architect of the "Great Society"— Lyndon Johnson was a complicated man for complicated times.

Sworn into the nation's highest office aboard Air Force One, Johnson found himself in the discomfiting position of realizing his long-held presidential aspirations in the face of devastating national tragedy: the cold-blooded murder of his predecessor and the enveloping cloak of mourning, chaos, and stasis that followed. Never entirely at ease in J.F.K.'s administration, whose inner circle he was not a part of, Johnson nonetheless took it upon himself to advance Kennedy's agenda, steering the civil-rights bill through Congress (where Johnson had served a dozen years in the House and a dozen more in the Senate) and escalating U.S. involvement in South Vietnam's battle against the Communist North.

This latter inheritance from Kennedy would cast a pall over Johnson's presidency, for the war he really wished to prosecute was his self-declared "War on Poverty": an ambitious array of social programs that addressed education, health care, crime, and urban quality of life. Indeed, Johnson muscled through an astonishing number of these and other initiatives, such as Medicare and Medicaid, that were part of his Great Society vision of an America protected by a benevolent Big Government. The Civil Rights Act of 1964, it turned out, was his legislative masterstroke, and its passage by Congress was a courageous and hard-won victory for Johnson, who knew that in backing the bill he ran the risk of forever alienating his Southern Democrat allies, to say nothing of his foes. Irascible and vulgar though he may have been—Johnson was not averse to cussing out his staff, picking up a pet beagle by its ears, or lifting up his shirt to show reporters a surgical scar—his concern for human rights was authentic.

But Johnson's standing suffered for his pledge not to be "the president who saw Southeast Asia go the way China went." His commitment of ever greater numbers of U.S. troops to Vietnam, for a war that seemed to grow more pointless and less winnable every year of his presidency, proved his political undoing. By March 1968, facing a home front ablaze with massive anti-war protests, Johnson declared himself unwilling to run for a second full term—making him, to date, the last eligible sitting president to opt out of an election.　　　　　　　　　　—D.K.

36~L. Johnson

37

RICHARD MILHOUS NIXON
1913–1994

PRESIDENCY, 1969-1974

At California's Whittier College, Richard Nixon was a brainy debater, an athlete, a Quaker Sunday-school teacher. But he soon morphed into a Republican pit bull, attending Duke Law and then, as a California congressman, embarking on a crusade to prove that Alger Hiss, a former aide to F.D.R., was a Soviet spy—which, it turned out, he may well have been. By 1952, Senator Nixon would be Ike's attack-dog running mate and would save his own political neck with his "Checkers" speech, in which Nixon rebuffed charges of improperly accepting gifts, strumming TV viewers' heartstrings with shout-outs to his beloved wife, Pat, and the family pooch, Checkers.

Nixon's presidential reign was framed by his futile attempts to reverse America's failed policy of "containing" Communism in Southeast Asia. He tried: Vietnamization (reducing U.S. troop levels yet financially bolstering South Vietnam) *plus* secret bombings (which his aides lied about to Congress and the country) *plus* peace talks. All the while, however, Nixon and his foreign-policy partner Henry Kissinger were busy plotting an aggressive, unified approach to global affairs—a mix of Realpolitik, shuttle diplomacy, and détente. Their breakthroughs were remarkable. They opened U.S. channels to the U.S.S.R. and China. They made genuine progress in scaling back nuclear arms. And despite Nixon's anti-Semitic rants, which would surface in Oval Office audiotapes he clandestinely recorded, the president and Kissinger backed Israel in the 1973 Yom Kippur War, helping to save the Jewish state. They also propped up pro-American regimes while destabilizing pro-Soviet ones.

At home, Nixon played to his base, envisioning a "silent majority" who considered wrenching social change to be a threat to the nation's core (read: conservative) values. But change he did, spurred by a Democratic Congress to create the Environmental Protection Agency, and supporting the Equal Rights Amendment, affirmative action, and food stamps. None of this, ultimately, helped his Q rating. No president (until George W. Bush, that is) was so widely eviscerated in popular culture, from scathing impressions by comedians to campus protesters wearing "Tricky Dick" masks.

A textbook paranoid, Nixon set loose a pack of operatives who targeted, spied on, and intimidated his "enemies." Indeed, during the Watergate affair—the most divisive White House scandal since Andrew Johnson's day—key Nixon advisers were revealed to have engaged in a systematic campaign of dirty tricks and political espionage, then to have conspired to obstruct justice by misleading or strong-arming investigators in efforts to cover their tracks. Come 1974, an occasionally discombobulated Nixon, who would hold drink-fueled encounter sessions with the West Wing's portraits of past presidents, resigned in disgrace. In all, some two dozen administration or campaign associates would cop guilty pleas or be convicted of Watergate-related crimes.

                                                                              —D.F.

37- Nixon·

38

GERALD RUDOLPH FORD
1913–2006

PRESIDENCY, 1974–1977

K nown for his fair dealings across his twenty-five years in Congress, Gerald Ford was the only person to hold the offices of vice president and president without having been elected to either. Although a longtime friend of the man who appointed him as his number two—upon the forced resignation of the legally beleaguered Spiro Agnew—Ford was the antithesis of Richard Nixon, which is to say he was straightforward and open, and he went by the book.

Three hours after escorting a shaken Nixon to that farewell helicopter on the South Lawn, Ford delivered brief remarks upon taking over. "My fellow Americans," he said, "our long national nightmare is over." In his first week as president, the nation began to heal as the low-key Ford—a Nebraska-born Republican who'd come to prominence as a Michigan legislator and well-respected U.S. House minority leader—slept at his modest home in the Virginia suburbs. Photographers captured him, still in his pajamas, picking up the morning paper from the stoop.

Americans responded to his decency, endorsing his offer of amnesty to Vietnam War–era draft dodgers, only to blanch when he pardoned Nixon a month into office. The newspapers smacked him around, and senators on the left and right howled: Ted Kennedy, the Massachusetts Democrat, called the move "a betrayal of the public trust," while Arizona Republican Barry Goldwater remarked, "It just doesn't make any sense."

Against the advice of Secretary of State Henry Kissinger, Ford next ordered the withdrawal of U.S. troops from Vietnam. War was over, at long last, but its end came with televised footage of Americans fleeing Saigon as it fell. Next on the agenda: a baffling economy (marked by steep inflation and energy challenges) and an attempt at reaching a nuclear-arms treaty with the Soviets, even as Ford supported the Helsinki Accords to confront human-rights abuses in the U.S.S.R. and Eastern Europe.

Ford's image took a direct hit when the president was portrayed as an oaf in an absurdist impression by *Saturday Night Live* player Chevy Chase. Few seemed to remember that a youthful, photogenic Jerry had appeared in picture spreads in *Life* and *Cosmopolitan*. Or that he'd been offered contracts by the Green Bay Packers and Detroit Lions upon his graduation from the University of Michigan, which he turned down to attend law school at Yale. Or that he had earned ten battle stars during World War II.

Before his death, in 2006, Ford was celebrated for his bipartisanship and his backbone. He was awarded the Presidential Medal of Freedom, and Ted Kennedy conceded that Ford had been wise, after all, in pardoning Nixon. The music played at his funeral couldn't have been more fitting: Aaron Copland's "Fanfare for the Common Man."

—J.W.

38-Ford·

James Earl Carter
1924-

PRESIDENCY, 1977-1981

Three decades before Barack Obama made the leap from near obscurity to the Oval Office, Jimmy Carter entered the 1976 campaign as a bona fide underdog, with little nationwide name recognition, few power-broker cronies in the capital, and not even much sway in his home state of Georgia.

He grew up in a house that had no running water or electricity. After a tour on nuclear submarines in the peacetime navy, Carter returned to Plains, Georgia, with his wife, Rosalynn, and took over the family business of farming, storekeeping, and peanut warehousing. With racial tensions flaring, a local group called the White Citizens Council asked him to join their cause. Carter angrily refused. After serving in the state senate, he ran a losing race for governor. A period of reflection followed, during which he listened to Bob Dylan, studied the writings of Christian activist Reinhold Niebuhr, and sought strength in his deepening Baptist faith. He won the next gubernatorial election and made the cover of *Time* in 1971 as the face of the New South, in part because of his bold assertion that "the time for discrimination is over."

As the 1976 presidential campaign unfolded, voters began to warm to this down-home, born-again Democratic outsider. He was sworn in as Jimmy Carter (rather than James Earl Carter Jr.) and carried his own travel bag when he boarded Air Force One. Although he won the diplomatic battle to turn over the Panama Canal to the locals, finessed an unlikely peace between Egypt and Israel in the Camp David Accords, and decried the Soviet military presence in the Persian Gulf and Afghanistan, his approval numbers slipped to thirty percent. He couldn't crack an economy suffering from "stagflation" or persuade the nation of the need for a radically revised energy policy. Carter tried to rouse the Republic with a speech titled "Energy and the Crisis of Confidence"—later derided as his "malaise speech"—but the tactic tanked. Soon after came the Iranian hostage crisis, in which Islamist students held fifty-two American diplomats in Tehran for the final four hundred forty-four days of the Carter presidency. A botched attempt to rescue the captives in a surprise military raid ended in carnage on a remote staging ground in Iran's Great Salt Desert. The recriminations soon followed.

The citizenry made an about-face, replacing the liberal and pious peanut farmer with a glamorous, twice-married conservative. But Carter went on to a remarkable post-presidential career, writing twenty books while working as an advocate for social justice, a Habitat for Humanity carpenter, and an observer of elections in far-flung trouble spots. In 2002 he became the third of four presidents to receive the Nobel Peace Prize.

—J.W.

39 - Carter

RONALD WILSON REAGAN
1911–2004

P R E S I D E N C Y , 1 9 8 1 – 1 9 8 9

His upbringing had a presidential patina: rural-Illinois childhood; summer lifeguard stints; a robust nickname—Dutch. Yet Ronald Wilson Reagan would soon develop the least likely résumé of any occupant of 1600 Pennsylvania Avenue: radio announcer for Chicago Cubs games (he'd read newswire updates of the on-field action, then pretend to do the play-by-play); B-movie actor (*King's Row, Hellcats of the Navy*), who portrayed football coach George "The Gipper" Gipp and, in *Bedtime for Bonzo,* a chimp's companion; divorcé (he split from actress Jane Wyman, in 1949, then married actress Nancy Davis).

But with his clout as the head of the Screen Actors Guild and the backing of a Kitchen Cabinet of high-powered California friends, the onetime Democrat developed his political chops, becoming the conservatives' darling, the Republican governor of the most populous state in the nation, and the ideal president for the historical moment. He understood Americans' affinity for glamour, for bromides, for conspicuous consumption. (The go-go eighties were propelled, in part, by his party's instinctual disdain for high taxes, regulation, and big government.) In an era of imagery, the Great Communicator employed a crack P.R. team and favored the photo op and the quick quip. Even after surviving a 1981 assassination attempt, he had a W. C. Fields line handy at the hospital: "All in all, I'd rather be in Philadelphia."

Where others had tried quiet diplomacy in foreign affairs, Reagan initially played the hard-nosed gunslinger, mirroring his political soulmate, Britain's Margaret Thatcher. But over time history would reward his more measured approach in his face-to-face dealings with his Russian counterpart, Mikhail Gorbachev. By decade's end, Reagan's insistence on developing an ill-fated space-based anti-missile system would help lead, counter-intuitively, to strategic-arms reductions. His assistance to the Afghan mujahideen would undermine Russia's military (though it would lead to blowback in the emergence of radical Islamist groups such as the Taliban and al-Qaeda). And his policies, and those of his successor, would contribute to the collapse of the U.S.S.R. and the entire Soviet bloc. Not bad for eight years' work—with an invasion of Grenada thrown in for good measure.

Reagan's second term was tarnished by his seemingly diminished attention span (he left office at age seventy-eight and was diagnosed with Alzheimer's four years later) and a tendency to over-delegate (during the Iran-contra crisis, his underlings were caught diverting weapons and funds to the Nicaraguan opposition—and to Iranian middlemen who claimed they could help free American hostages held in Lebanon). Yet he always had a guiding star, quite literally. The First Lady, to chart her husband's fortunes, dutifully consulted astrologer Joan Quigley, who would later boast, "I helped end the Cold War." —D.F.

40-Reagan·

— № 41 —

GEORGE HERBERT
WALKER BUSH
1924–

PRESIDENCY, 1989–1993

Patrician by birth and Texan by choice, Bush spent his political career trying to reconcile his privileged New England background (Massachusetts-born, Connecticut-reared) with the homespun populism that had come to define the Republican Party. His single term in office, beginning as it did at the tail end of the eighties, is often described as "Ronald Reagan's third term"—an apt summation of the bind that history and his lineage placed him in. Reagan was the more charismatic politician, and indeed thwarted Bush's own presidential aspirations in 1980, but Bush was the one with the more impeccably Establishment résumé.

The second son of Prescott Bush, a two-term U.S. senator from Connecticut, George was educated at Phillips Academy and Yale University. As such, he had the locutions and pastimes of a New England prepster: avidly golfing and speedboating at the family's summer compound in Maine, asking for "a splash more coffee" at a truck stop. But political ambition and a desire to escape his family's shadow found him staking out a new identity as an oil wildcatter in West Texas.

From this new, southern base, Bush built an impressive political portfolio, first serving as a congressman and then, in the 1970s, becoming U.S. ambassador to the United Nations, chairman of the Republican National Committee, chief U.S. liaison to China, and director of the Central Intelligence Agency.

Yet all this experience couldn't entirely negate what *Newsweek* memorably called "the wimp factor"—the perception that Bush was a coddled Little Lord Fauntleroy, somehow not man enough to follow Reagan. (This tag deeply irritated him, especially given that he had survived being shot down over the Pacific as a navy pilot during World War II.)

As president, Bush was quickly presented with opportunities to prove his manhood. He sent U.S. troops into Panama to depose the dictator Manuel Noriega; basked in reflected glory as the Berlin Wall fell and devoted his considerable diplomatic skills to the orderly dismantling of the Soviet empire; and oversaw Operation Desert Storm, the quick and successful trouncing of the Iraqi troops that Saddam Hussein had sent to invade oil-rich Kuwait.

His Persian Gulf War triumph augured an easy re-election in 1992, but Bush seemed blindsided by the economic recession that arose in the conflict's aftermath, paving the way for the first Democratic president in twelve years, one William Jefferson Clinton. Still, Bush stepped down with grace and characteristic good humor, quoting Winston Churchill's line from 1945: "I have been given 'the Order of the Boot.'"   —D.K.

41 - G.H.W.Bush

WILLIAM JEFFERSON CLINTON
1946-

PRESIDENCY, 1993-2001

Both his strengths and his flaws were outsize, and from his earliest days, Bill Clinton once said, he knew that politics was the "only track I ever wanted to run on." For eight rollicking years of comparative peace and extraordinary prosperity, he carried his country along on a wild ride.

The son of a traveling salesman, who died before he was born, and of a mother who was married a total of five times to four men, he swallowed up life in great, heaping gulps. He looked for love in all the right places (especially from the voters) and many of the wrong ones too. Governor of his native Arkansas at thirty-two (the youngest in the nation), Clinton won the presidency in an improbable three-way race (against incumbent Bush and businessman Ross Perot, an independent). Then, after overreaching in his bid to reshape the health-care system, he promptly lost Democratic majorities in Congress, putting the G.O.P. in control of both houses for the first time in forty years.

Always at his best when on the ropes, Clinton the brawler clawed his way back anyhow, becoming the first Democrat elected to a second full term since F.D.R. But he soon put everything at risk for a secret affair with a White House intern barely half his age. The exposure of his deceptions, midway through his second term, led ill-advised Republicans in Congress to make him the second president ever to be impeached. His job-approval ratings, astonishingly, only grew with his legal bills, and he was acquitted at trial in the Senate.

In foreign affairs, he coaxed the heads of Israel and the Palestine Liberation Organization to shake hands on the White House lawn (though their historic Oslo Accords would fray and dissolve), helped broker a fragile peace in Northern Ireland, and ultimately forced an end to murderous "ethnic cleansing" in Bosnia and Kosovo. At home, he oversaw a turbocharged economy, championed social-parity initiatives such as the Family and Medical Leave Act, and instituted sweeping welfare reform.

The youngest former president since Teddy Roosevelt, he remained active—even hyperactive—on the national and world stages. If his efforts to make his wife and longtime political partner, Hillary Rodham Clinton, the first female president backfired, it seems safe to say that his tenure (and talents) helped pave the way for the election of Barack Obama, whose administration was heavily staffed with veterans from Clinton's deep bench.   —T.S.P.

42~Clinton·

GEORGE WALKER BUSH
1946-

PRESIDENCY, 2001-2009

Sworn into office under contentious circumstances—he'd lost the popular vote in the 2000 election to Vice President Al Gore and prevailed in the Electoral College only after a five-to-four Supreme Court ruling put a halt to a protracted Florida recount—the eldest son of the forty-first president was nevertheless welcomed into Washington as an affable centrist: a popular, Connecticut-born governor of Texas who, in his bonhomie and religious conviction, would provide a welcome respite from the rancor and messiness of the Clinton era.

This was not to be. Thanks to a tight inner circle of advisers sometimes known as the Vulcans, after the Roman god of fire—Vice President Dick Cheney chief among them—the Bush administration very quickly veered hard right. Most significantly, in 2003, it hustled the U.S. military into a costly and bloody invasion of Iraq, squandering much of the international goodwill toward America that had arisen in the aftermath of the horrific attacks of September 11, 2001.

Bush's initial response to those attacks, which had been hatched by Afghanistan-based operatives of the Islamist terrorist leader Osama bin Laden, was admirable: he reassured a populace in shock and provided a firm hand at the helm as he sent forces to kill or capture bin Laden and expel his Taliban protectors. But the administration's fixation on Iraqi dictator Saddam Hussein, and its dubious attempt to connect him to the 9/11 attacks, soon saw the U.S. diverting troops and resources from the task at hand. While the Iraq war did succeed in rousting Hussein from power, its otherwise ineffectual prosecution signaled a lack of competence and intellectual rigor at the top. The Bush team compounded its troubles with a slow-motion response to Hurricane Katrina, which ravaged New Orleans in 2005, killing eighteen hundred residents and leaving four hundred thousand homeless. The deep recession of 2008, its seeds sown by years of look-the-other-way fiscal policy, was, for many, the final nail in the president's political coffin.

Bush could take credit for legitimate accomplishments, not least his establishing safeguards that arguably secured the mainland from a subsequent assault and his oft overlooked redoubling of U.S. efforts in the global fight against AIDS. But by the time he left office, in 2009, his popularity was the lowest ever for any outgoing president, and his infamous May 2003 photo op aboard the U.S.S. *Abraham Lincoln*—in which he stood before a banner bearing the words MISSION ACCOMPLISHED and announced that "major combat operations in Iraq have now ended"—had become a bitter symbol of a president clearly out of sync with the times. —D.K.

43~J.W.Bush

BARACK HUSSEIN OBAMA
1961-

A rise that once seemed improbable now seems inevitable, and a presidency that loomed as exceptional quickly came to be taken for granted. It is Barack Obama's singular gift, and special burden, that whatever he ends up doing in the White House, he has already made history of the first order by getting there.

The son of a Kenyan economist and a Kansan anthropologist, Obama was born and came of age in Hawaii, the newest state, at a time when interracial marriage was illegal in much of the mainland. Throughout his life, he has been on the leading edge of social and cultural change. As a boy, he struggled to find his identity, but as a man he found it in full measure, as a community organizer on the South Side of Chicago, capital of the American black diaspora, and as the first black president of the *Harvard Law Review*. He chronicled this journey in *Dreams from My Father,* surely the most personal presidential memoir ever written.

Eventually, he saw practical politics as the surest route to meaningful change, and he won a seat in the Illinois State Senate. Propelled from obscurity by his 2004 Democratic-convention keynote speech ("There's not a liberal America and a conservative America; there's a *United States* of America"), he came to Washington as a U.S. senator, and, almost before he'd had time to unpack, began running for president, boosted by a bestselling book, a knack for oratory, and a commitment to civility. Against all odds, he built the biggest, richest campaign organization in American history and defeated Hillary Rodham Clinton, heir to the most powerful Democratic brand name in a generation, to win the nomination. His Republican opponent, war hero John McCain, never seemed to know what hit him.

President Obama inherited a plateful of economic and national-security problems as grave as any since the Great Depression, and he resolved to address them with an eye firmly on the long game, even as his message experts tried to carefully calibrate the daily news cycle. In his first year in office, Obama shifted the nation's main military focus (from Iraq to Afghanistan and Pakistan) and its financial focus as well (introducing sweeping measures to shore up embattled industries and stimulate the blighted economy). He sought—not always successfully—to build bridges with Republicans in Congress and to hit the reset button on foreign policy and health care. Eight months into his presidency, he received the Nobel Peace Prize for his "extraordinary efforts to strengthen international diplomacy and cooperation between peoples."

Obama's critics have attacked his bona fides, his tendency to take on too much, and his belief in big government, but he brushes them off. He has always worn his ambition lightly; he is driven, without seeming to be so. His stylish wife and two little girls have brought a grace and glamour to the White House not seen since the days of J.F.K. His story is unfinished, but his nation is already changed.   —T.S.P.

44·Obama·

PRESIDENTS

- on -

THEIR PREDECESSORS

———

ON THE FOLLOWING PAGES, EACH AMERICAN PRESIDENT
OFFERS HIS FRANK ASSESSMENT OF THE MAN WHO IMMEDIATELY PRECEDED
HIM AS COMMANDER IN CHIEF

JOHN ADAMS
on GEORGE WASHINGTON
– 1812 –

"Among the national sins of our country |is| the idolatrous worship
paid to the name of George Washington by all classes and nearly all parties of
our citizens, manifested in the impious applications of names and epithets
to him which are ascribed in scripture only to God and to Jesus Christ.
The following is a part of them: 'our Savior,' 'our Redeemer,' 'our cloud by day
and our pillar of fire by night,' 'our star in the east,' 'to us a Son is born,'
and 'our guide on earth, our advocate in heaven.'"

THOMAS JEFFERSON
on JOHN ADAMS
– 1788 –

"He is vain, irritable and a bad calculator of the force and
probable effect of the motives which govern men. This is all
the ill which can possibly be said of him."

JAMES MADISON
on THOMAS JEFFERSON
– 1826 –

"|He was| more than consoled for the loss by the gain to him, and by
the assurance that he lives and will live in the memory and gratitude of the wise
and good, as a luminary of science, as a votary of liberty, as a model of
patriotism, and as a benefactor of the human kind."

JAMES MONROE
on JAMES MADISON
– 1831 –

"I deeply regret . . . that there is no prospect of our ever meeting again,
since so long have we been connected, and in the most friendly intercourse,
in public and private life, that a final separation is among the most
distressing incidents which could occur."

JOHN QUINCY ADAMS
on JAMES MONROE
– 1825 –

"Thus strengthening and consolidating the federative edifice of his
country's Union, till he was entitled to say, like Augustus Caesar of his imperial
city, that he had found her built of brick and left her constructed of marble."

ANDREW JACKSON
on JOHN QUINCY ADAMS
– 1831 –

"What disgraceful scenes in congress. . . . Is Mr. Adams demented, or is he
perversely wicked. Both, I think, and Adams ought to be confined to a hospital."

MARTIN VAN BUREN
on ANDREW JACKSON
– 1854 –

"I never knew a man more free from conceit, or one to whom it was
a greater extent a pleasure, as well as a recognized duty, to listen patiently what
might be said to him upon any subject."

WILLIAM HENRY HARRISON
on MARTIN VAN BUREN
– 1841 –

"It was the remark of a Roman consul, in an early period of that
celebrated republic, that a most striking contrast was observable
in the conduct of candidates for offices of power and trust,
before and after obtaining them—|men such as Van Buren| seldom
carrying out in the latter case the pledges and promises
made in the former."

JOHN TYLER
on WILLIAM HENRY HARRISON
– 1841 –

"The death of William Henry Harrison, late President of the United States,
so soon after his elevation to that high office, is a bereavement
peculiarly calculated to be regarded as a heavy affliction, and to impress all
minds with a sense of the uncertainty of human things, and of the dependence
of nations, as well as individuals, upon our Heavenly Parent."

JAMES KNOX POLK
on JOHN TYLER
– 1841 –

"|Tyler deserves| the lasting gratitude of his country |for| arresting
the dominant majority in Congress in their mad career, and saving his country
from the dominion and political incubus of the money-power in the
form of a National Bank."

ZACHARY TAYLOR
on JAMES KNOX POLK
– 1848 –

"If elected I would not be the mere president of a party."

MILLARD FILLMORE
on ZACHARY TAYLOR
– 1850 –

"I have no language to express the emotions of my heart.
The shock |of his death| is so sudden and unexpected, I am overwhelmed."

FRANKLIN PIERCE
on MILLARD FILLMORE
– 1853 –

"I believe that involuntary servitude, as it exists in different States of
this Confederacy, is recognized by the Constitution. I hold that the laws
|of my predecessor|, commonly called the 'compromise measures,'
are strictly constitutional."

JAMES BUCHANAN
on FRANKLIN PIERCE
– 1852 –

"It is his peculiar distinction, above all other public men within my knowledge,
that he has never had occasion to take a single step backwards."

ABRAHAM LINCOLN
on JAMES BUCHANAN
– 1861 –

"Mr. President, I cannot say that I shall enter it with much pleasure,
but I assure you that I shall do what I can to maintain the high standards set
by my illustrious predecessors who have occupied it."

ANDREW JOHNSON
on ABRAHAM LINCOLN
– 1864 –

"His sole object has been to save what his country's enemies would destroy.
In my judgment, Mr. Lincoln, as President and Commander-in-Chief,
has done naught, not perfectly justifiable and constitutional."

ULYSSES S. GRANT
on ANDREW JOHNSON
– 1885 –

"He delivered a speech of welcome.... It was long, and I was in torture while he
was delivering it, fearing something would be expected of me in response.
I was relieved, however, the people assembled having apparently heard enough."

RUTHERFORD BIRCHARD HAYES
on ULYSSES S. GRANT
– 1865 –

"Grant however rules matters where he really attempts it."

JAMES ABRAM GARFIELD
on RUTHERFORD BIRCHARD HAYES
– 1878 –

"The policy of the President has turned out to be a give-away from
the beginning. He has nulled suits, discontinued prosecutions,
offered conciliation everywhere in the South, while they have spent their
time in whetting their knives for any Republican they could find."

CHESTER ALAN ARTHUR
on JAMES ABRAM GARFIELD

– 1881 –

"The hideous crime which has darkened our land, and the memory
of the murdered President, his protracted sufferings, his unyielding fortitude,
the example and achievements of his life, and the pathos of his death
will forever illuminate the pages of our history."

GROVER CLEVELAND
on CHESTER ALAN ARTHUR

– 1885 –

"The people demand reform in the administration of the Government and
the application of business principles to public affairs."

BENJAMIN HARRISON
on GROVER CLEVELAND

– 1888 –

"In the passage of what is now so flippantly called the war tariff,
to raise revenue to carry on the war out of the protective duties which were
then levied, there has come to this country a prosperity and
development which would have been impossible without it, and that reversal of
this policy now, at the suggestion of Mr. Cleveland, according to
the line of the blind statesman from Texas, would be to stay and interrupt
this march of prosperity on which we have entered."

GROVER CLEVELAND
on BENJAMIN HARRISON

– 1901 –

"In public office he was guided by patriotism and devotion to duty—
often at the sacrifice of temporary popularity—and in private station his
influence and example were always in the direction of decency
and good citizenship. Such a career and the incidents related to it should leave
a deep and useful impression upon every section of our national life."

WILLIAM McKINLEY
on GROVER CLEVELAND

– 1885 –

"What in the world has Grover Cleveland done? Will you tell me?
You give it up? I have been looking for six weeks for a Democrat who could
tell me what Cleveland has done for the good of his country and for
the benefit of the people, but I have not found him."

THEODORE ROOSEVELT
on WILLIAM McKINLEY

– 1896 –

"McKinley, whose firmness I utterly distrust[,] will be nominated;
and this . . . I much regret."

WILLIAM HOWARD TAFT
on THEODORE ROOSEVELT
– 1916 –

"My judgment is that the view of . . . Mr. Roosevelt, ascribing an undefined residuum of power to the President is an unsafe doctrine, and that it might lead under emergencies to results of an arbitrary character, doing irremediable injustice to private rights."

WOODROW WILSON
on WILLIAM HOWARD TAFT
– 1913 –

"The idea of the Presidents we have recently had has been that they were Presidents of a National Board of Trustees |the Cabinet|. . . . I want to be President of the people of the United States."

WARREN GAMALIEL HARDING
on WOODROW WILSON
– 1912 –

"|Wilson| is a clean, learned, honorable, and patriotic man."

CALVIN COOLIDGE
on WARREN GAMALIEL HARDING
– 1923 –

"He caught the ear of a war-tired world. He called our country back to paths of peace and gladly it came."

HERBERT CLARK HOOVER
on CALVIN COOLIDGE
– 1933 –

"Mr. Coolidge was a real conservative, probably the equal of Benjamin Harrison. . . . Any summation of Mr. Coolidge's services to the country must conclude that America is a better place for his having lived in it."

FRANKLIN DELANO ROOSEVELT
on HERBERT CLARK HOOVER
– 1932 –

"I accuse the present Administration of being the greatest spending Administration in peace times in all our history. It is an Administration that has piled bureau on bureau, commission on commission, and has failed to anticipate the dire needs and the reduced earning power of the people."

HARRY S. TRUMAN
on FRANKLIN DELANO ROOSEVELT
– 1941 –

"He's so damn afraid that he won't have all the power and glory that he won't let his friends help as it should be done."

DWIGHT DAVID EISENHOWER
on HARRY S. TRUMAN
– 1953 –

"Truman didn't know any more about government than
a dog knows about religion."

JOHN FITZGERALD KENNEDY
on DWIGHT DAVID EISENHOWER
– 1960 –

"That old asshole."

LYNDON BAINES JOHNSON
on JOHN FITZGERALD KENNEDY
– 1969 –

"Here was a whippersnapper.... He never said a word of importance
in the Senate and he never did a thing. But somehow . . . he managed to create
the image of himself as a shining intellectual, a youthful leader
who would change the face of the country."

RICHARD MILHOUS NIXON
on LYNDON BAINES JOHNSON
– 1978 –

"I think that Lyndon Johnson died of a broken heart, physically
and emotionally. He was an enormously able and proud man. He desperately
wanted, and expected, to be a great President. He drove himself
to outdo his predecessor. After I won the election in 1968, and through the
remaining years of Johnson's life, I saw what some have described as
the 'better side' of his character. He was courteous, generally soft-spoken, and
thoughtful in every way. He was not the pushing, prodding politician
or the consummate partisan of his earlier career. Above all Johnson wanted
to be loved—to earn not only the approval but also the affection of
every American. Much of his overblown rhetoric and many of his domestic
policies were rooted in this compulsive quest for approbation."

GERALD RUDOLPH FORD
on RICHARD MILHOUS NIXON
– 1994 –

"One minute he was outgoing, extrovert, the next reflective, even sullen.
My impression was that his moodiness drained a lot out of him."

JAMES EARL CARTER
on GERALD RUDOLPH FORD
– 1976 –

"I think this Republican administration has been almost all style, and
spectacular, and not substance.... As far as foreign policy goes, Mr. Kissinger
has been the President of this country."

RONALD WILSON REAGAN
on JAMES EARL CARTER
– 1980 –

"We must overcome something the present administration has cooked up:
a new and altogether indigestible economic stew, one part inflation,
one part high unemployment, one part recession, one part runaway taxes,
one part deficit spending, seasoned by an energy crisis."

GEORGE HERBERT WALKER BUSH
on RONALD WILSON REAGAN
– 2002 –

"There was a kindness there that taught me a good lesson—
don't get to be a big deal, don't bawl out the airline stewardess, don't throw
your weight around. Contain your anger. Smile a lot. Laugh.
Be kind to people. Those values I learned from Ronald Reagan.
He was a beautiful, beautiful man in that sense."

WILLIAM JEFFERSON CLINTON
on GEORGE HERBERT WALKER BUSH
– 1992 –

"This President got there not with a vision but by first taking out
his primary opponents and then taking out his general-election opponent."

GEORGE WALKER BUSH
on WILLIAM JEFFERSON CLINTON
– 2000 –

"It's time to restore honor and dignity to the White House."

BARACK HUSSEIN OBAMA
on GEORGE WALKER BUSH
– 2008 –

"These |economic| challenges are not all of government's making.
But the failure to respond is a direct result of a broken politics in Washington
and the failed policies of George W. Bush."

———

PRESIDENTS
- in -
MINT CONDITION

ON BILLS

$1 — GEORGE WASHINGTON

$2 — THOMAS JEFFERSON

$5 — ABRAHAM LINCOLN

$20 — ANDREW JACKSON

$50 — ULYSSES S. GRANT

$500 — WILLIAM MCKINLEY

$1,000 — GROVER CLEVELAND

$5,000 — JAMES MADISON

$100,000 — WOODROW WILSON

ON COINS

PENNY — ABRAHAM LINCOLN

NICKEL — THOMAS JEFFERSON

DIME — FRANKLIN DELANO ROOSEVELT

QUARTER — GEORGE WASHINGTON

50-CENT PIECE — JOHN FITZGERALD KENNEDY

DOLLAR COIN* — DWIGHT DAVID EISENHOWER

NON-PRESIDENTS REPRESENTED

$10 — ALEXANDER HAMILTON
(FEDERALIST CHAMPION; TREASURY SECRETARY)

$100 — BENJAMIN FRANKLIN
(FOUNDING FATHER; AMERICAN ICON)

$10,000 — SALMON P. CHASE
(TREASURY SECRETARY; CHIEF JUSTICE OF THE SUPREME COURT)

*By 2016, all deceased presidents will have been depicted on a dollar coin
as part of an initiative by the U.S. Mint.*